# BOOKS UNDER FIRE

# BOOKS UNDER FIRE

## A hit list of banned and challenged children's books

**PAT R. SCALES**

*for the Office for Intellectual Freedom*

An imprint of the American Library Association
Chicago   |   2015

**PAT SCALES** is a retired middle and high school librarian whose programs have been featured on the *Today Show* and in various professional journals. She received the ALA/Grolier Award in 1997, and has served as chair of the prestigious Newbery, Caldecott, and Wilder Award committees. She is a past president of the Association of Library Service for Children, a division of the American Library Association. Scales has been actively involved with ALA's Intellectual Freedom Committee for a number of years, is a member of the Freedom to Read Foundation, serves on the Council of Advisers of the National Coalition Against Censorship, and acts as a spokesperson for First Amendment issues as they relate to children and young adults. She is the author of *Teaching Banned Books: Twelve Guides for Young Readers* and *Protecting Intellectual Freedom in Your School Library*. She writes a bimonthly column for *School Library Journal*, a monthly column for the Random House website, and is a regular contributor to *Book Links* magazine.

© 2015 by the American Library Association
Printed in the United States of America

19  18  17  16  15    5  4  3  2  1

Extensive effort has gone into ensuring the reliability of the information in this book; however, the publisher makes no warranty, express or implied, with respect to the material contained herein.

ISBN: 978–0-8389–1109–9 (paper).

**Library of Congress Cataloging-in-Publication Data**
Scales, Pat.
　　Books under fire : a hit list of banned and challenged children's books /
　　Pat Scales.
　　　　pages  cm
　　Includes bibliographical references and index.
　　ISBN 978-0-8389-1109-9
　　1. Challenged books—United States—Bibliography. 2. Prohibited books—
　United States—Bibliography. 3. Children's literature—Censorship—United
　States. 4. School libraries—Censorship—United States. 5. Children—Books and
　reading—United States. I. Title.
Z1019.S325 2015
016.098'10973—dc23

　　　　　　　　　　　　　　　　　　　　　　　　　2014023945

Book design by Kim Thornton in the Charis SIL and Proxima Nova typefaces.

♾ This paper meets the requirements of ANSI/NISO Z39.48–1992
(Permanence of Paper).

*This book is for*

Judy Blume, Beverly Horowitz
*and*
Cynthia Samuels

*The three who were there in the very beginning*
*supporting my work with intellectual freedom*

*Thank You*
*My Free Speech Sisters*

# Contents

IN "THE WILDERNESS OF CHILDHOOD," MICHAEL CHABON DESCRIBES HIS happy Maryland boyhood environs—alleys, friends' houses, vacant lots, and playgrounds. So, too, Chabon read books that took him to new neighborhoods outside his comfort zone. He mourns that today's youth have lost that opportunity to explore:

> The thing that strikes me now when I think about the Wilderness of Childhood is the incredible degree of freedom my parents gave me to adventure there. A very grave, very significant shift in our idea of childhood has occurred since then. The Wilderness of Childhood is gone; the days of adventure are past. The land ruled by children, to which a kid might exile himself for at least some portion of every day from the neighboring kingdom of adulthood, has in large part been taken over . . .
>
> What is the impact of the closing down of the Wilderness on the development of children's imaginations? This is what I worry about the most. I grew up with a freedom, a liberty that now seems breathtaking and almost impossible. (Michael Chabon, "The Wilderness of Childhood," in *Manhood for Amateurs* [New York: HarperCollins, 2009], 59–66.)

I am proud to introduce you to Pat Scales, the author of this new book. Pat walks the walk and talks the talk. She has been there—on the front lines, defending and promoting the freedom to read for children. As a school librarian she used books to help students make sense out of the "wilderness" of contemporary society, and to develop their creative and critical skills. She has published countless articles, columns, guides, and books about how to use "edgy," controversial books to introduce young people to uncomfortable ideas. Ideas they will need for their school days and for the workplace ahead of them. And for the sheer pleasure and "shock of recognition" in engaging with complex ideas and characters they can relate to.

Pat's book will show you how to embrace, not avoid, acclaimed books that children love. By teaching these books in your classroom, library, or home, you are there to engage with children if they want to discuss parts of the book that puzzle them. And you will find that these books often touch upon those very issues that young people are experiencing. These books should not frighten us; they are a tool for opening up dialogue and programming for public libraries as well.

Unfortunately, the American Library Association's Office for Intellectual Freedom receives hundreds of complaints, and actual removals of books from school and public libraries, every year. Please consider reporting book challenge incidents to the ALA Office for Intellectual Freedom at www.ala.org/bbooks/challengedmaterials/reporting. All reports are kept confidential if you so wish. We use this data to discern trends in censorship so that we can support books like this one!

I hope that this book will show a different path through the wilderness—opening it up for exploration, thought, and discussion instead of closing it off.

*Barbara M. Jones*
*Director, ALA Office for Intellectual Freedom*
*April 28, 2014*

**IT'S EASY TO BECOME INTIMIDATED WHEN SOMEONE APPEARS AT THE DOOR**
of a school or public library and challenges a book. But librarians and
teachers develop more courage to face these challenges once they learn
that there is a community of professionals and tools to assist them. The
American Library Association's (ALA) Office for Intellectual Freedom
(OIF) offers a number of services, including strategies for dealing with
challenges, tips for talking with the media, and when appropriate, they
may even put librarians who have dealt with challenges in touch with one
another.

Challenges or questions regarding the content in children's books
are very common, but rarely do they result in book banning. No public or school library is immune from those who want to deny children's
access to certain books and materials. This is why all libraries must have
a "materials selection policy" that includes procedures for dealing with
challenges. When procedures are followed, the library almost always ends
up the winner. Trouble erupts when librarians, school administrators, or
library directors bypass the appropriate procedure for the sake of avoiding
a "civic debate." News about controversial books spreads like gossip, and
an attempt to cover up challenges may actually result in a "public uproar."

This actually happened when PABBIS (Parents Against Bad Books in
Schools) attacked a long list of books in Fairfax, Virginia. One vocal par-

ent called for the school board to "prevent this unnecessary and harmful wave of censorship." The president of the student body at Thomas Jefferson High School spoke passionately about students' right to read. Once the school administration and school board allowed the school district's selection policy to become their armor, they won the battle and the books remained in the school libraries. A similar public outcry occurred when the state of Arizona banned the Mexican-American Studies Program in the Tucson Unified School District. Books, including *Mexican WhiteBoy* by Matt de la Peña, were boxed and marked BANNED. Students were so angry that they invited de la Peña to come to Tucson to speak. These readers fought and won, and de la Peña awarded them the best possible prize—copies of his book. The Mexican-American Studies Program was reinstated three years later.

In 1993, copies of *Annie on My Mind* (1982) by Nancy Garden were burned in Olathe, Kansas, because of the "homosexual" theme. The superintendent of schools removed the book from the junior high and high school libraries without due process because he wanted to "avoid controversy." That's actually when the controversy began. Four students sued the school district on grounds that their First Amendment rights had been violated. The case went to trial in 1995, and the students and the book won. This happened because articulate students convinced the judge of the book's value, and because the school board had violated their own materials selection and reconsideration policies. The school district did not appeal the judge's decision, and the book was returned to library shelves.

In each of these cases, the Office for Intellectual Freedom and the Freedom to Read Foundation provided assistance and moral support, and in some cases legal support, to the students, their parents, and the school librarians. Attempts to censor books that kids read shouldn't be hidden. When played out in full view, there are parents and children who are willing to speak loudly about children's free speech rights, and there are a host of professional librarians, writers, lawyers, and organizations eager to help.

The Office for Intellectual Freedom maintains a database of challenged materials and regularly compiles and publishes a list of these titles. This is an effort to put book challenges front and center so that librarians and the public are aware of these attempts to abridge an individual's freedom to read. Many of the books on these lists are children's books. The titles in *Books under Fire: A Hit List of Banned and Challenged Children's Books* are taken from the ALA's records, as well as challenged titles collected by the Texas ACLU, the Oregon Intellectual Freedom Clearinghouse, and the National Council of Teachers of English. Some of the titles in this book have been featured in *Hit List for Children: Frequently Challenged Books for Children 2* (2002), but they are included here because they have recent challenges. *Blubber* by Judy Blume, *Julie of the Wolves* by Jean Craighead George, and *Scary Stories to Tell in the Dark* by Alvin Schwartz are among the books that continue to be challenged.

The Association of Library Service to Children (ALSC) serves library users from birth to age 14, and the Young Adult Library Services Association (YALSA) provides programs and services for ages 12–18. Since there is a two-year overlap, and because young adolescents read both children's and teen books, some of the titles in this book may also be ones that YALSA has included in some of their publications on censorship and intellectual freedom.

*Books under Fire: A Hit List of Banned and Challenged Children's Books* is meant to be a resource for librarians and teachers for their own professional growth, and to use as a tool to help young readers become aware of the social issues that are most often at the center of the majority of book challenges for children. The featured titles appear in alphabetical order by author. For each title, there is a summary of the book, or series; quotes from professional review sources and dates of reviews; the details of recorded challenges; Awards (like Newbery and Caldecott and State Children's Book Awards) and Accolades (like ALSC Notable Children's Books List and *Booklist* Editor's Picks); Official Website for the author/illustrator or publisher; Further Reading which includes print and digital resources about the author, the book, and censorship; and For Listening and Viewing, which includes recorded links to interviews with the writer/illustrator of the book and related videos and movies available on the Internet.

The final two sections for each entry have not been included in the previous *Hit List* books. Talking with Readers about the Issues provides open-ended age-appropriate questions for librarians to use with classes, children's book clubs, library-sponsored reading groups, and parents. The questions focus on specific reasons for the books' challenges and are intended to engage readers in good conversation about the entire books rather than taking words or scenes out of context. When young readers learn to think, state their opinions, and listen to the thoughts of others, they are likely to embrace the content in a mature manner. They may even be insulted that some adults have attempted to deny them access to the books. Illustrations help tell the story in picture books. For this reason, questions for picture books like *And Tango Makes Three* and *The Dirty Cowboy* also call upon readers to connect visually to the story. In books like *My Mom's Having a Baby* and *It's Perfectly Normal,* the illustrations have collected as many challenges as the text.

Recommended Books That Have Been Challenged for Similar Reasons offers two or three suggestions of books that have been challenged in public and school libraries based on the same issues. Some of these books were actually challenged many decades in the past. This is intended to reveal trends in book censorship, and how concerns like "profanity," "sexual content," "violence and horror," and "religious viewpoint" are identical to the ones the Office for Intellectual Freedom have dealt with since they began tracking book challenges.

There are several appendixes: (A) Resources for Teaching Young Readers about the First Amendment; (B) Bibliography: Professional Resources about Book Censorship and the Freedom to Read; (C) Rankings of Children's and Young Adult Books in the Top 100 Most Banned or Challenged Books List: 2000–2009; (D) Children's Classics and Why They Have Been Challenged; (E) Caldecott Medal and Honor Books: Why They Have Been Challenged; and (F) John Newbery Medal and Honor Books: Why They Have Been Challenged.

Librarians and teachers have a responsibility to protect children's right to read, but professionals also have the responsibility to promote these rights. This is quite possibly the best assurance that each generation of readers truly understands what it means to be intellectually free.

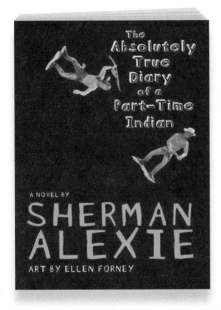

*Sherman Alexie*

## The Absolutely True Diary of a Part-Time Indian

*Illustrated by Ellen Forney.*
*New York: Little, Brown Books*
*for Young Readers, 2007*

FOURTEEN-YEAR-OLD ARNOLD SPIRIT JR. LIVES AND ATTENDS SCHOOL ON THE Spokane Indian Reservation in Washington State. The reservation is riddled with poverty, and there is very little to eat in most households. The school resorts to used and outdated textbooks, and most students have no aspirations or goals for the future. Junior, as Arnold is called, is a good basketball player and artist, and he needs to get out. Life has been especially tough for him. He was born with "water on the brain," and his odd looks make him the ideal target of bullies. To make matters worse, he stutters, suffers from frequent seizures, and has very poor eyesight. Some of the bullies on the reservation think he looks and acts like the cartoons he draws.

Alcoholism is rampant on the reservation, and Junior's family is no exception. His parents are drunk most of the time, and his sister, who does manage to get off the reservation, dies in a mobile home fire because she was too drunk to smell the smoke. The most positive role model in his life is Grandmother Spirit. Junior is devastated when she is hit and killed by a drunk driver while walking home from a powwow. She and Junior enjoyed a special relationship, and it is she who provided him advice and support.

Rowdy, Junior's best friend, is tough and tries to protect him from the bullies. But he can't assist Junior with the pent-up anger raging inside his head. At the beginning of Junior's freshman year in high school, he sees his mother's name in a math textbook and becomes so angry about the age of the book that he throws it and breaks the teacher's nose. This act of violence is a turning point for him. The teacher, known as Mr. P, realizes that Arnold has potential and encourages him to get off the reservation and create a better life for himself. To some on the reservation, Junior is abandoning his own culture when he enrolls in an all-white high school twenty-two miles away in Reardan. Now called Arnold, he struggles to fit in. There are times when his part-time life on the reservation and his part-time life in a school filled with spoiled rich kids do collide. He faces prejudices against Indians at school, and he is the only one enrolled, and back home his status as a "traitor" makes him an outcast among his own people. Things turn around for him when he makes the high school basketball team, develops a crush on a popular white girl, and makes friends with a school geek who becomes his mentor.

Told in first person from Arnold's point of view, his story contains sixty-five "comic-style" illustrations that contribute to both the humorous and tragic parts of his story as he struggles to bridge two very different cultures.

*School Library Journal* (September 1, 2007) says the book "delivers a positive message in a low-key manner." They recommend it for grades 7–10. Ian Chipman, the reviewer for *Booklist* (August 1, 2007), states that Alexie "doesn't pull any punches as he levels his eye at stereotypes both warranted and inapt." *Kirkus* (July 15, 2007) calls the novel an "achingly clear-eyed look at the realities of reservation life." *Publishers Weekly* (August 20, 2007) comments on the "dark humor" and the "jazzy syntax and Forney's witty cartoons." *Horn Book Magazine* (September 1, 2007) recommends the book for middle and high school students and calls "Junior's spirit unquenchable and his style inimitable." A teen reviewer for *Voice of Youth Advocates* (August 1, 2007) says that the novel is "realistic and fantastical and funny and tragic all at the same time." Bruce Barcott, the reviewer for the *New York Times Sunday Book Review* (November 11, 2007), states that the novel is "a gem of a book." He praises Alexie by saying that this "may be his best work yet." *The Guardian* (October 3, 2008) praises the book and says, "It's humane, authentic and, most of all, it speaks."

## CHALLENGES

According to data collected by the ALA's Office for Intellectual Freedom, Alexie's novel was #3 on the Top Ten Most Frequently Challenged Books List in 2013, #2 in 2012; #5 in 2011; and #2 in 2010. The reasons cited include "drugs/alcohol/smoking, offensive language, racism, sexually explicit, unsuited to age group."

A parent objected to the book in Crook County, Oregon, in 2008 because of references to "masturbation." The book was removed from the library shelves.

In 2009 the novel was retained on the summer reading list at Antioch (Illinois) High School despite objections from several parents who found the book "vulgar" and "racist."

The book was banned in the curriculum, but retained in the library at the Newcastle (Wyoming) Middle School in 2010. In the same year, the school board in Stockton, Missouri, voted to ban the book. In the same year, the novel was challenged at Helena High School in Montana. The challenge was withdrawn under pressure from the Montana ACLU.

The novel was challenged, but later returned to the Richland, Washington, school district in 2011 because of "coarse themes and language." In the same year, it was pulled from the Dade County, Georgia, library shelves and the required high school reading list because of complaints of "vulgarity, racism, and anti-Christian content." It was also challenged at the Old Rochester Regional Junior High School in Mattapoisett, Massachusetts, as an eighth-grade English assignment.

There were challenges to the novel as required reading in at least three freshman English classes at the Westfield (New Jersey) High School in 2012 because of "very sensitive material in the book including excerpts on masturbation amongst other explicit sexual references, encouraging pornography, racism, religious irreverence, and strong language (including the f-and n-words)." The school board voted to retain the book. In the same year, the novel was challenged in the Geraldine, Montana, public schools as "inappropriate for classroom because of sex and language." The status of the challenge is unknown. The novel was also challenged, but retained in the Springfield, Massachusetts's public schools. The Comic Defense Fund aided in this defense.

In 2013 the novel was banned at Public School 114 (middle school) in Rockaway, Queens, New York, because the topic of "masturbation" isn't "appropriate for eleven year olds."

The novel was banned in the Meridian (Idaho) high school in 2014 because it "contains language we do not speak in our homes." It was challenged, but retained in the Billings (Montana) School District 2.

## AWARDS AND ACCOLADES

2010  California Young Reader Medal: Young Adult
2009  Delaware Diamonds Book Award: High School
2009  Great Lakes Great Book Award: Grades 9–12 (Michigan)
2008  Washington State Book Award
2008  *Boston Globe-Horn Book* Award: Fiction
2008  ALA/YALSA Best Books List
2007  National Book Award for Young People's Literature
2007  *New York Times* Notable Books: Children's Books
2007  *Publishers Weekly* Best Children's Books List
2007  *Publishers Weekly* Best Books of the Year List
2007  *School Library Journal* Best Books of the Year List

## AUTHOR'S OFFICIAL WEBSITE

http://fallsapart.com

## FURTHER READING

### Author/Illustrator

"Ellen Forney." *Contemporary Authors* online, 2014. Books and Authors. Gale

"Sherman Alexie." *Contemporary Authors* online, 2012. Books and Authors. Gale.

### Book

Alexie, Sherman. "Fiction and Poetry Award Winner: The Absolutely True Diary of a Part-Time Indian" (speech). *Horn Book Magazine* 85 (January/February 2009): 25–28.

Alexie, Sherman. "Why the Best Children's Books Are Written in Blood." *Wall Street Journal,* June 9, 2011. http://blogs.wsj.com/speakeasy/2011/06/09/why-the-best-kids-books-are-written-in-blood.

Alexie, Sherman. "How to Fight Monsters." *Read* 57 (February 8, 2008): 20–24.

Crandall, Bryan Ripley. "Adding a Disability Perspective When Reading Adolescent Literature: Sherman Alexie's *The Absolutely True Diary of a Part-Time Indian.*" *Alan Review* 179 (Winter 2009): 71–78.

Hunt, Jonathan. "Worth a Thousand Words." *Horn Book Magazine* 84 (July/August 2008): 421–26.

Insenga, Angela. "Taking Cartoons as Seriously as Books: Using Images to Read Words in *The Absolutely True Diary of a Part-Time Indian.*" *SIGNAL Journal* 35 (Spring/Summer 2012): 18–26.

Macintyre, Pamela. "The Rise of the Illustrated Young Adult Novel: Challenges to Form and Ideology." *International Journal of the Book* 8 (2011): 135–43.

## Censorship

Bousquet, Mark. "Sherman Alexie: Censorship of Any Form Punishes Curiosity." *Comic Book Legal Defense Fund,* October 15, 2012. http://cbldf.org/2012/10/sherman-alexie-censorship-of-any-form-punishes-curiosity.

Connelly, Joel. "Sherman Alexie Novel Banned in Meridian, Idaho." *Seattlepi.com,* April 3, 2014. http://blog.seattlepi.com/seattlepolitics/2014/04/03/sherman-alexie-novel-banned-in-meridian-idaho.

"Sherman Alexie Talks to NCAC's The Write Stuff about Being Banned." February 19, 2013. http://ncacblog.wordpress.com/2013/02/19/sherman-alexie-talks-to-ncacs-the-write-stuff-about-being-banned.

## For Listening and Viewing

www.youtube.com/watch?v=LUs9Boyqqdc. May 22, 2013. Sherman Alexie talks to the American Booksellers for Free Expression.

www.c-span.org/video/?202083-3/book-discussion-absolutely-true-diary-parttime-indian. November 3, 2007. Sherman Alexie speaks at the 2007 Texas Book Festival.

**TALKING WITH READERS ABOUT THE ISSUES**

- Analyze the title of the book. At what point in the novel do you recognize the meaning of "part-time"? Why is it so difficult for Arnold to be "part-time" in the two worlds in which he lives?
- Alexie opens a window for readers when he reveals the character of Junior and details his life on the reservation. What do you see? Why is it important to have an open mind when reading about other cultures, people, or environments that are different from yours?
- How does Alexie use humor to soften the "dark" side of Junior's life? Explain how the cartoon illustrations contribute to the novel. How do they expand the text?
- This novel has been challenged and banned because of "offensive language, drugs/alcohol/smoking, sex, and racism." How are these issues a very real part of Junior's life? Why is talking about these issues better than denying that they exist?
- How is the novel about courage and hope? Focus on these themes and prepare a statement in defense of the novel.

**RELATED BOOKS CHALLENGED FOR SIMILAR REASONS**

*Aquado, Bill, ed.* **Paint Me Like I Am: Teen Poems from WritersCorps.** *New York: HarperTeen, an imprint of HarperCollins, 2003.*

In 2009 the principal at the Landis Intermediate School in Vineyard, New Jersey, removed two pages that included the poem "Diary of an Abusive Step-Father" after a thirteen-year-old Landis student's mother questioned its appropriateness. The thirty-one-line poem is peppered with profanity and details a violent relationship between an adult and child. San Francisco-based WritersCorps, an art organization linking writers with teens in urban areas to provide outlets for their experiences, produced the anthology.

It was also challenged in 2009 in the combined middle and high school library in the North Fond du Lac School District in Wisconsin. The book was retained provided it has a label designating it as appropriate for high school students. Younger students could also access the book with prior parental permission.

*Chbosky, Stephen.* **The Perks of Being a Wallflower.** *MTV/ Pocket Books, an imprint of Simon and Schuster, 1999 (reissued 2012).*

This coming-of-age novel, written in a series of letters from the main character to an anonymous character, was #9 on the American Library Association's Top Ten Frequently Challenged Books List in 2009. It has been challenged and banned because of frank descriptions of "masturbation, sex, drugs and suicide." It has also been labeled offensive for reasons related to "religious viewpoint and anti-family." Somewhat autobiographical, Chbosky says that he wrote the book at a time when he was dealing with some teen trauma.

*Avi*

# The Fighting Ground

*New York: HarperCollins, 1984*

THIRTEEN-YEAR-OLD JONATHAN'S OLDER brother is fighting with General Washington in Pennsylvania while Jonathan is stuck on the family farm near Trenton, New Jersey, doing chores alongside his father. More than anything, Jonathan wants to fight the British, but his father insists that he is too young to go to war. When the tavern bells rings, Jonathan knows the sound means that men are being called to fight. On April 3, 1778, at exactly 9:58 A.M., the bell tolls and Jonathan's father sends him to seek news. Jonathan gets there and finds an American corporal rallying local men to form an army. Jonathan is recruited, loaned a musket by the tavern owner, and before he realizes what is happening he is in the middle of a battle and taken prisoner by three Hessian soldiers. As he contemplates escape, Jonathan wonders where he will go. He's not sure he can return to the farm since he didn't listen to his mother and disobeyed his father. He's not even sure he can return to the tavern since he no longer has the owner's gun. He has even failed the Corporal, who finally realizes that Jonathan is just a boy. Jonathan does have the opportunity to shoot the Hessians, but there has already been too much bloodshed, and he doesn't know if he can kill. Instead he tries to warn them that the Corporal is outside the house where they are hiding. The Hessians in turn use Jonathan as a human shield, but he manages to run to safety. This all occurs within a 24-hour period. When Jonathan does make it home, he finds that his life has changed in ways he never expected.

Susan F. Marcus, reviewer for *School Library Journal* (September 1984), says, "The author points up the harshness of his subject with appropriate severity of language." B*ooklist* (June 1, 1984) thinks the book is "a vivid telling of a brief and intensely personal moment of history." *Boys Life* (October 1984) summarizes the novel in "About Books" and says, "right and wrong are not as easy to tell apart in the middle of a battle." *Horn Book Magazine* (June 1984) says Avi "skillfully captures Jonathan's physical and emotional experiences."

## CHALLENGES

The ALA's Office for Intellectual Freedom reports that the novel is #43 on the 2000–2009 Top 100 Most Banned/Challenged Books.

In 2000 the book was challenged, but retained as part of the John Fuller School curriculum in Conway, New Hampshire, despite a complaint by a resident calling himself a concerned Christian.

In the 2003–2004 school year the novel was challenged, but retained in the Harmony Elementary School in San Antonio, Texas, because of "profanity and inappropriate language."

According to the 2005–2006 Texas ACLU Report of Banned and Challenged Materials, there was a challenge to Avi's novel at the Reeces Creek Elementary School in the Killeen Independent School District for "profanity/inappropriate language." The word "Goddamnit" was blacked out and the book remained on the shelf. In the same year, the novel was challenged in the curriculum for "drunkenness, gruesome death, references to alcohol" at the New Boston Middle School in the New Boston Independent School District in Texas. An alternate book was allowed.

In 2008 the novel was banned from the shelves of the Bay District school libraries in Panama City, Florida, after a parent noted several profanities uttered by some soldiers.

## AWARDS AND ACCOLADES

1985   Jefferson Cup Award Honor Book, Virginia Library Association
1984   Scott O'Dell Award: Best Historical Fiction
1984   ALA Notable Children's Books
1984   ALA Best Books for Young Adults
1984   ALA Hi-Lo Books
1984   Notable Children's Trade Books in Social Studies

## AUTHOR'S OFFICIAL WEBSITE

www.avi-writer.com

## FURTHER READING

### The Author

"Avi." *Contemporary Authors online.* 2013. Books and Authors. Gale

Harvey, Mary. "Advice from Avi." *Scholastic Scope* 51 (January 24, 2003): 21.

Marinak, Barbara Ann. "Author Profile: Avi." *Book Report* 10 (March/ April 1992): 26–28.

Mercier, Cathryn M. *Presenting Avi.* Farmington Hills, MN: Cengage Gale, 1997. 228 p. (Twayne's United States Authors Series)

Somers, Michael A. *Avi.* New York: Rosen Publishing Group, 2004. 112 p. (The Library of Author Biographies Series)

Weisman, Kay. "Talking with Avi." *Book Links Magazine,* a publication of *Booklist* 18 (July 2009): 40–42.

Yuan, Margaret. *Avi.* New York: Facts on File, 2005. 112 p. (Who Wrote That? Series)

### The Book

Avi. "The Child in Children's Literature." *Horn Book Magazine* 69 (January/February): 40–51.

White, Georganne. "Fabulous Fiction with Good Elementary Social Studies Connections." *Emergency Librarian* 20 (September/October 1992): 29.

### Censorship

Avi. "Young People, Books, and the Right to Read." *Journal of Youth Services in Libraries* 6 (Spring 1993): 245–54.

Wollman-Bonilla, Julie E. "Outrageous Viewpoints: Teachers' Criteria for Rejecting Works of Children's Literature." *Language Arts* 75 (April 1998): 287–95.

**For Listening and Viewing**

www.youtube.com/watch?v = 1j1RgRJ-0qYU. AdLit, January 24, 2011.
Avi talks about himself as a student and how his teachers responded
to him.

www.youtube.com/watch?v = OBIDvuWHnuk. *Reading Rockets,* August 4,
2010. In this interview with *Reading Rockets,* Avi talks about writing
and its challenges.

## TALKING WITH READERS ABOUT THE ISSUES

- What is Jonathan's father's attitude toward the war? Why is Jonathan so intent on fighting?
- Those who challenge the novel are offended by the language, and don't think that books for young readers should contain obscenities. How is the language in the novel the language of war?
- The novel has also been challenged because of "violence." Discuss how the violence in the novel is necessary to realistically depict what Jonathan is experiencing.
- Jonathan disobeys his father and joins the Colonel's army. Why is returning to the farm and facing his father difficult for him?
- How does the war change Jonathan?

## RELATED NOVELS CHALLENGED FOR SIMILAR REASONS

*Forbes, Esther.* **Johnny Tremain.** *Boston: Houghton Mifflin Harcourt, 1943.*

This 1944 Newbery Medal Book was challenged because of "violence" in North Carolina in 2001. The library requested that the challenge remain private.

*Paulsen, Gary.* **Woods Runner.** *New York: Wendy Lamb Books, an imprint of Penguin Random House, 2010.*

In 2011 this novel set during the American Revolution was removed from an optional reading list in Oregon because of "violence." The library wished to remain private.

*Judy Blume*

# Blubber

*New York: Bradbury, 1974;*
*reissued by Macmillan, 2006*

JILL BRENNER, THE NARRATOR, IS IN THE fifth grade at Hillside Elementary School in a well-to-do suburb. She wants so badly to be in the "popular crowd" that she loses sight of what is right and wrong. When Linda Fischer, an overweight classmate, gives an oral science report on whales, Wendy, the most popular girl in the class, passes a note that says, "Blubber is a good name for her!" Mrs. Minish, the teacher, doesn't have complete control of the class and only makes idle threats about the girls' behavior. The teasing and name calling continues on the school bus when another group of girls tortures Linda by singing "Blubbery blubber. . . . blub, blub, blub, blub. . . ." to the tune of "Beautiful Dreamer." Then the boys get involved and the bullying gets completely out of hand. At times, Jill shows signs of being uncomfortable with the way Linda is treated, but her desire to please Wendy is just too strong, and she soon becomes a ringleader.

On Halloween, Jill dresses as a flenser (one who strips blubber off whales), and is disappointed when she doesn't win the costume contest. The judges were not impressed, but Wendy and her followers take great notice, and appoint Jill, the flenser, the task of stripping Blubber of her clothing. The gang gathers in the girls' restroom and holds Blubber down while Jill attempts to undress her. Though the girls never accomplish their task, they do manage to reveal Linda's "flowered underpants."

Things begin to change for Jill when her family goes to Warren Winkler's bar mitzvah and she is seated at the table with Linda. To Jill's surprise, she and Linda are asked to light the thirteenth candle on Warren's birthday cake. But there is still some question about who squealed on Jill and her friend, Tracy, for putting raw eggs in Mr. Machinist's mailbox on Halloween. Wendy tries to convince the girls that Linda is the guilty party and instigates a mock trial, but doesn't give Linda a lawyer. Jill finally gets sick of Wendy and her bossy ways, and declares, "If Blubber doesn't get a lawyer then Blubber doesn't go on trial."

Jill realizes she was acting mean not because she is mean, but because of the pressure of fitting in. She never learns that it is wrong to persecute someone; she simply learns that once the tables are turned, it really hurts.

*School Library Journal* (November 1974) says the novel "realistically portrays under-twelve social dynamics." *The Bulletin of the Center for Children's Books* (May 1975) says that Judy Blume tells the story with a "respectful and perceptive understanding of the anguished concerns of the pre-teen years." *Kirkus* (October 1, 1974) states that Blume "presents the scenes of viciousness without commentary." A young reader posted a review on Amazon (November 6, 2001) and called out other reviewers who are troubled by the novel, "I'm in sixth grade and guess what? Real life is like this book."

## CHALLENGES

According to the ALA's Office for Intellectual Freedom, the novel was #30 on the 100 Most Frequently Challenged Books 1990–1999, and was ranked #43 on the Top 100 Most Challenged/Banned Books 2000–2009. To date, the American Library Association has recorded challenges in Alabama, California, Colorado, Delaware, Georgia, Illinois, Indiana, Kentucky, Nebraska, New Jersey, New York, North Carolina, Ohio, and Texas.

The earliest recorded challenge was in 1980 when the novel was removed from all library shelves in the Montgomery County (Maryland) elementary schools.

In 1983 it was challenged at the Xenia (Ohio) school libraries because the book "undermines authority since the word 'bitch' is used in connection with a teacher." In the same year, it was also challenged at the Smith Elementary School in Del Valle, Texas, because of the words "damn" and "bitch" and it "showed children cruelly teasing a classmate."

It was banned in 1984, but later restricted to students with parental permission at the Peoria (Illinois) School District because of its strong "sexual content and language, and alleged lack of social or literary merit." In the same year, it was restricted at the Lindenwold, New Jersey, elementary school libraries because of "a problem with language." It was also removed from the Hanover (Pennsylvania) School District's elementary and secondary libraries, but later placed on a "restricted shelf" at middle school libraries because it was considered "indecent and inappropriate."

In 1985 it was challenged as "profane, immoral, and offensive," but retained in the Bozeman, Montana, school libraries.

A challenge was recorded in 1986 at the Muskego (Wisconsin) Elementary School because "the characters curse and the leader of the taunting is never punished for her cruelty." The result of the challenge is unknown.

In 1991 it was challenged at the Perry (Ohio) Township elementary school libraries because the "bad is never punished. Good never comes to the fore. Evil is triumphant."

The novel was banned at Clements High School in Athens, Alabama, in 1998 because of objections to two uses of "damn" and "bitch." The decision was later reversed.

In 1999 it was removed from an elementary school in Arlington, Texas, because educators objected to "verbal, physical, and sexual abuse of student upon student."

The book was challenged in a school library in Colorado in 2002 because it was deemed "unsuited for age group." In the same year, it was challenged at a school in New York for unspecified reasons. The institutions asked that the details of the challenges remain "private." The status of the challenges is unknown.

In 2004 there was a challenge at a school in Georgia because it was considered "unsuited for age group." In the same year, it was challenged in a school library in Texas because of "offensive language." The specifics of the challenges are "private" at the request of the institution. The status of the challenges is unknown.

In 2005 a teacher in a school in Indiana challenged the book because of "offensive language." The school requested to remain "private." The status of the challenge is unknown.

According to the 2012–2013 Texas ACLU Report of Challenged and Banned Materials, the novel was challenged at the Lake Dallas Elementary School because of "profanity." The book was not a part of the library collection, but in a "Guided Reading" classroom. It was retained, but restricted to fifth graders.

## AWARDS AND ACCOLADES

1983  Flicker Tale Children's Book Award (North Dakota)
1977  Arizona Young Readers Award
1977  Pacific Northwest Library Association Young Readers Choice Award
1974  *New York Times* Outstanding Book of the Year

## AUTHOR'S OFFICIAL WEBSITE

www.judyblume.com

## FURTHER READING

### The Author

Bohning, Patricia, and Ann Keith Nauman. "Judy Blume: The Lady and the Legend" (bibliographical essay). *Emergency Librarian* 14 (November/December 1986): 17–20.

Gottlieb, Amy. "Judy Blume." *Jewish Women: A Comprehensive Historical Encyclopedia.* March 1, 2009. http://jwa.org/encyclopedia/article/blume-judy.

Jones, Jen. *Judy Blume: Fearless Storyteller for Teens.* Berkeley Heights, NJ: Enslow, 2008. 112 p. (Authors Teens Love Series)

"Judy Blume." *Contemporary Authors* online, 2009. Books and Authors. Gale.

Ludwig, Elisa. *Judy Blume.* New York: Chelsea House, 2003. 112 p. (Who Wrote That? Series)

Maynard, Joyce. "Coming of Age with Judy Blume." *New York Times,* December 3, 1978. www.nytimes.com/books/98/09/13/specials/maynard-blume.html.

Weidt, Maryann N. *Presenting Judy Blume.* Farmington Hills, MN: Cengage Gale, 1989. 168 p. (Twayne United States Authors Series)

### The Book

www.nytimes.com/books/98/09/13/specials/maynard-blume.html.
http://bookshelvesofdoom.blogs.com/bookshelves_of_doom/2006/05/blubber_judy_bl.html.

## Censorship

Brancato, Robin F. "In Defense of: *Are You There God? It's Me, Margaret,* *Deenie,* and *Blubber*–Three Novels by Judy Blume." In *Censored Books: Critical Viewpoints,* ed. Nicholas J. Karolides, John M. Kean, and Lee Burress. Metuchen, NJ: Scarecrow, 1993, pp. 87–97.

"Censorship in Children's Books" (symposium). *Publishers Weekly* 232 (July 24, 1987): 108–11.

Dillin, Gay Andrews. "Judy Blume: Children's Author in a Grown-up Controversy." *Christian Science Monitor,* December 10, 1981. www.csmonitor.com/1981/1210/121061.htm.

www.indexoncensorship.org/2013/09/judy-blume-banned-books.

## For Listening and Viewing

www.youtube.com/watch?v = 91eJiPqVOAM. AdLit., January 24, 2011. Judy Blume talks about childhood memories of visiting the library, and the importance of books in the lives of children.

www.youtube.com/watch?v = fuhp3VTQQ2Q. ALA/OIF, September 7, 2011. Judy Blume talks about censorship for the Banned Books Week Virtual Read-Out.

## TALKING WITH READERS ABOUT THE ISSUES

- Why is Linda such an easy target for bullies like Wendy?
- Describe Mrs. Minish, the fifth-grade teacher. Why doesn't she notice that something is going on with the girls? What advice would you give her?
- The novel has been challenged and banned because of "bullying." How realistic is the novel? How should one deal with a bully?
- The novel has also been banned because of "profanity." Read the passage on page 95 where Jill talks about cursing, and discuss whether her observation about why people use bad language is true. What is an appropriate response to someone who uses bad language to your face?
- One of the challenges to *Blubber* concerns the perception that in the book "bad is never punished. Good never comes to the fore. Evil is triumphant." Debate whether evil is really triumphant in the novel. The book is about Jill, not Wendy or Linda. What lessons does Jill learn about evil? How is Jill triumphant?

## RELATED NOVELS CHALLENGED FOR SIMILAR REASONS

Choldenko, Gennifer. **Al Capone Does My Shirts.** *New York: G. P. Putnam Sons, an imprint of Penguin Random House, 2004.*

According to the Texas ACLU, this Newbery Honor book was challenged in the school year 2008–2009 at the Childress Elementary School in the Childress Independent School District because of "profanity." Moose, the main character, also deals with Piper, the warden's daughter, who breaks the rules of Alcatraz and gets Moose in trouble.

Cole, Brock. **The Goats.** *New York: Farrar, Straus and Giroux, an imprint of Macmillan, 1987.*

This novel was #26 on the American Library Association's 100 Most Frequently Challenged Books List: 1990–1999 because of "language and nudity." The main characters are labeled "outcasts" which makes them the targets of extreme bullying at the camps they are attending.

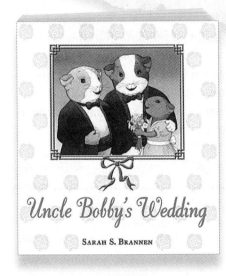

*Sarah S. Brannen*

# Uncle Bobby's Wedding

*New York: G. P. Putnam's Sons, an imprint of Penguin Random House, 2008*

**CHLOE, A YOUNG GUINEA PIG, IS UPSET WHEN SHE LEARNS THAT UNCLE BOBBY,** her favorite uncle, is getting married. She and her uncle have fun together, doing things like strolling through the woods and rowing on the river. Now she is worried that Uncle Bobby will no longer have time for her. When Chloe's mom has a picnic to celebrate Uncle Bobby's engagement to his male friend Jamie, Chloe is too sad to enjoy the day. At her mother's suggestion, Chloe and Uncle Bobby have a long talk. Uncle Bobby assures her that they can still have fun together. To prove to her that she is a part of his new life, he and Jamie invite her for ice cream, take her sailing, and at the end of a long day together, they roast marshmallows in the fireplace. Then Uncle Bobby and Jamie ask Chloe to be the flower girl in their wedding. Chloe puts on her new dress, her mother puts the finishing touches on the wedding cake, and Chloe helps Uncle Bobby and Jamie get ready. When Uncle Bobby can't find the wedding rings, and Jamie can't tie his bow tie, Chloe comes to the rescue. The entire family gathers in the garden to watch Uncle Bobby and Jamie say their vows. "Everyone danced until the moon rose."

*School Library Journal* (April 1, 2008) recommends the book for K–Gr. 2 and states that Chloe's mother simply tells her, "people who love each other 'want to be married.'" Hazel Rochman, reviewer for *Booklist* (January 1, 2008), calls the book "a celebration of same-sex marriage." *Publishers Weekly* (January 7, 2008) says "the issue of same-sex marriage is incidental to the plot." *Kirkus* (February 1, 2008) states that the "fact of two men marrying is a refreshing nonissue here." And *The Bulletin of the Center for Children's Books* (January 2008) says that the book "reassures youngsters who are uneasy about family change."

## CHALLENGES

According to the ALA's Office for Intellectual Freedom, the book was #8 on the Top Ten Most Challenged Books list in 2008. It climbed to #4 on the Top Ten Most Challenged Books in 2012.

In 2008 there were two challenges at the Douglas County Public Library in Castle Rock, Colorado, because the "topic of gay marriage is inappropriate." The book was retained. In the same year, there were reported challenges because of the "homosexual" subject matter in public libraries in Maryland and Pennsylvania. The libraries asked that the details of the challenge remain private. The statuses of these challenges are unknown.

In 2010 there was a challenge filed in a Colorado public library because of the "homosexual theme." At the request of the library, the details of the challenge remain confidential. The status of the challenge is unknown.

The book was challenged in 2012 at the Brentwood Public Library in Missouri because "This book seeks to influence young children and to accept an activity that is illegal (homosexual) marriage, and a lifestyle that is well-documented to be harmful to one's physical and emotional well-being." The Library Board voted unanimously to retain the book.

" Children need to see families like theirs in the books they read, and there are over two million children being raised by same-sex parents in the US. I got plenty of hate mail, and read some dreadful things about myself on the Internet in the years following the publication of *Uncle Bobby's Wedding*. It wasn't fun, but I got wonderful letters too."

—Sarah Brannen, author of *Uncle Bobby's Wedding*

## AWARDS AND ACCOLADES

2009   SIRT (Social Issues Round Table) Rainbow Lists.

## AUTHOR'S OFFICIAL WEBSITE

www.sarah-brennan.com

## FURTHER READING

### The Author

Tenean, Kathy. http://kathytemean.wordpress.com/2012/07/21/
illustrator-saturday-sarah-brannen.

### The Book

Paccione-Dysziewski, Margaret R. "Same-Sex Relationships (and Other
Tricky Topics) in Children's Literature." *Brown University Child and
Adolescent Behavior Letter* 26 (December 2010): 8.

### Censorship

Gardner, Jan. "Squeals of Protest." *The Boston Globe*, September 20, 2009.
www.boston.com/ae/books/articles/2009/09/20/sarah_brannens
_uncle_bobbys_wedding_among_books_most_frequently_challenged.
http://jaslarue.blogspot.com/2008/07/uncle-bobbys-wedding.html.
http://cbldf.org/2012/11/challenge-to-uncle-bobbys-wedding-rejected
-in-missouri.

### For Listening and Viewing

www.youtube.com/watch?v=p75MElHqczo. September 27, 2013. A
child relates why *Uncle Bobby's Wedding* has been challenged, and
states her opinion of the book for the Banned Books Week Virtual
Read-Out.

## TALKING WITH READERS ABOUT THE ISSUES

- Why is Chloe sad that Uncle Bobby is getting married?
- Chloe doesn't ask any questions about Uncle Bobby marrying another man. Discuss whether she even notices. How does her mother explain the marriage to her?
- How do Uncle Bobby and Jamie let Chloe know that she is special to both of them?
- Chloe's family is very accepting of Uncle Bobby and Jamie's marriage. How do they celebrate the wedding?
- Explain how the book is about love.

## RELATED BOOKS CHALLENGED FOR SIMILAR REASONS

*De Haan, Linda, and Stern Nijand.* **King and King.** *Berkeley, California: Tricycle, a children's imprint of Ten Speed Press, 2002.*

This book was #20 on the American Library Association's 100 Most Banned/Challenged List 2000–2009. In 2004 the Association Press reported a challenge in a Wilmington (North Carolina) elementary school. When a first-grader borrowed the book from the school library, the mother filed a complaint and stated "My child is not old enough to understand something like this, especially when it is not our beliefs.

*Willhoit, Michael.* **Daddy's Wedding.** *New York: Alyson, 1996.*

The Oregon Intellectual Freedom Clearing House reports that this book was challenged, but retained in a public library because of the subject of "homosexuality." The library patron was concerned "that younger children might see the drawings of adult men kissing, which may lead to discussion that parents aren't ready for."

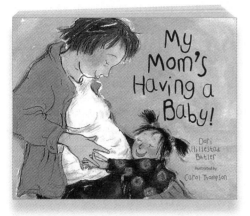

*Dori Hillestad Butler*

# My Mom's Having a Baby!

*Illustrated by Carol Thompson.*
*Morton Grove, Illinois: Albert*
*Whitman & Co., 2005*

**ELIZABETH IS EXCITED BECAUSE THERE IS A BABY GROWING INSIDE HER MOM.**
There is a long wait before she can meet the new baby because he has only been in her mom's uterus for four weeks. Elizabeth's mother is very open with her and tells her everything about the baby's development. As her mother's pregnancy progresses, Elizabeth has questions about how the baby got in her mom's tummy, and how he will get out. She learns that "the man puts his penis between the woman's legs and inside her vagina." Her mom explains about "the liquid that shoots out a man's penis" to fertilize the egg (proper anatomical terms are used). Elizabeth wonders about the sex of the baby and sees for herself that it is a boy when she goes with her mom for an ultrasound. Elizabeth understands that the baby is the result of "love-making," and when Michael is born the entire family celebrates the new addition.

Stephanie Zvirin, the reviewer for *Booklist* (April 1, 2005), recommends the book for grades 2–4 and comments on the "affectionate family dynamics" and notes that the "enthusiastic narration beautifully sustains the child-centric view." *School Library Journal* (May 1, 2005) calls the book "an excellent choice for those readers who are ready to ask and be told some of life's basic facts." The journal recommends the book for grades K–4. *Kirkus* (March 1, 2005) focuses on the "cartoon-style watercolors" and makes note that "Mom and Dad are under covers." The reviewer points out the numbers of "labeled inside views and enlargements."

**CHALLENGES**

The book was #4 on the American Library Association's Top Ten Most Challenged Books List in 2011.

The Oregon Intellectual Freedom Clearinghouse reported a challenge in 2006 in an "unnamed" public library because the "subject may rob children of innocence." The book was retained.

In 2008 the book was challenged at the Jessamine County Public Library in Nicolasville, Kentucky, for "sexual content." The result of the challenge is unknown.

In 2011 a woman in Carrollton, Texas, challenged *My Mom's Having a Baby* after a nine-year-old girl she was babysitting checked the book out of the public library. The babysitter contacted Fox News and the case was aired by affiliates nationwide. The babysitter took issue with the book because she didn't feel it appropriate for children. The story prompted additional challenges, including one at the Hillsborough County Public Library in Tampa, Florida. The author reports additional challenges in Indiana, Kansas, Colorado, and Georgia. Note: Some individuals reporting challenges to the American Library Association have asked to remain anonymous. The association honors such privacy.

**AWARDS AND ACCOLADES**

2005   *Booklist* Editor's Choice

" I appreciate that not everyone wants their children to have access to my book, but those people need to understand that there are other families who *do* want their children to have access to it. No one has the right to decide what should and should not be available for everyone else to read."

—Dori Hillestad Butler, author of *My Mom's Having a Baby*

## OFFICIAL WEBSITE

www.kidswriter.com/books.htm

## FURTHER READING

### The Author

"Dori Hillestad Butler." *Contemporary Authors* online, 2007. Books and Authors. Gale.

### Censorship

Butler, Dori Hillestad, guest, September 2, 2012. "Banned Books Month: Guest Post from Dori Hillestad Butler: How Censorship Has Changed Me." In *Write All the Words: Kristin Anderson Blog*. www.ekristin anderson.com/?p=7651.

Scales, Pat. "Talking with Dori Hillestad Butler." *Book Links,* A Supplement to *Booklist* 22, no. 1 (September 2012): 18–20. www.booklistonline.com/ProductInfo.aspx?pid=5551407.

http://mirishorten.blogspot.com/2012/10/my-moms-having-baby-kids-month-by-month.html.

### For Listening and Viewing

www.youtube.com/watch?v=wEh-mBfXxIQ. OpenRoadMedia Videos, July 7, 2011. This is a video profile of Dori Butler.

www.youtube.com/watch?v=yhMm1HSyZmM. ALA/OIF, October 1. This is Dori Butler's appearance for the 2012 Banned Books Week Virtual Read-Out.

## TALKING WITH READERS ABOUT THE ISSUES

- What does the cover of the book illustrate about Elizabeth's feelings toward her mom's pregnancy?
- Before reading the book, write down a list of questions that Elizabeth might ask her mom about the baby growing inside her.
- Elizabeth's mom is honest about how the baby got inside her. How does the baby represent love between Elizabeth's mom and dad?
- What does the ultrasound tell Elizabeth about the baby?

- Why is it called "labor" when a baby is ready to be born?
- Discuss what Elizabeth feels when she sees her baby brother for the first time. What are ways that she can help her mom when they bring the baby home from the hospital?

## RELATED BOOKS CHALLENGED FOR SIMILAR REASONS

*Brown, Laurie Krasny, and Marc Brown.* **What's the Big Secret: Talking about Sex with Girls and Boys.** *New York: Little, Brown, 2000.*

In 2001 the book was challenged, but retained at the Oak Harbor (Washington) School District No. 202 despite a parent's concern that the book discusses sex and "it's completely too graphic."

*Harris, Robie H.* **It's So Amazing: A Book about Eggs, Sperm, Birth, Babies and Families.** *Illustrated by Michael Emberley. Cambridge: Candlewick, 1999.*

This book was relocated to the reference section of the Northern Hills Elementary School library in Onalaska, Wisconsin, in 2005 because a parent complained about its frank yet kid-friendly discussion of reproduction topics, including sexual intercourse, masturbation, abortion, and homosexuality.

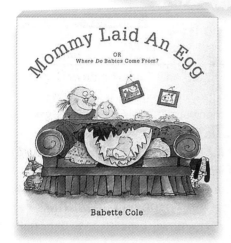

Babette Cole

# Mommy Laid an Egg! or, Where *Do* Babies Come From?

*San Francisco: Chronicle, 1993*

WHEN MOM AND DAD DECIDE IT'S TIME TO TELL JUNIOR AND HIS SISTER HOW babies are made, they go through a litany of explanations, from "sugar and spice and everything nice" (girls) to "slugs and snails and puppy dog tails" (boys). They explain that babies can be brought by dinosaurs, made out of gingerbread, found under stones, grown from seeds, or squeezed from tubes. But in their case "Mommy laid an egg." The children think the explanations are hilarious and they set their parents straight by drawing stick figures to illustrate "some ways mommies and daddies fit together." Such talk and illustrations make the parents blush, but the kids are perfectly at ease.

Cole's cartoon-like illustrations capture the nuances of life in a family where kids clearly rule the roost. Unlike some informational books in disguise as stories, this picture book is entertaining while pulling no punches about the basics of human reproduction. In a starred review, *Publishers Weekly* (June 7, 1993) calls Cole's sense of humor "endearingly loony" and her drawings and text "candid without being offensive." The reviewer for *Kirkus* (June 15, 1993) finds the book "a notably fresh, matter-of-fact approach." *Booklist* (July 1993) says, "In her own inimitable and illustrative style, Cole sets out to do what everyone wants to do—present an accessible, humorous, accurate look at where babies come from." The book is available in 72 languages and is the subject of discussion on a number of "Mommy Blogs."

## CHALLENGES

This book is among the American Library Association's Top 100 Banned Books: 1990–2000.

In 1998 the mother of an eight-year-old girl who checked the book out of the Camden County Library in Missouri objected to the book. The library board subsequently decided to move it and all other books dealing with sex education from the children's section to the adult section.

The Oregon Intellectual Freedom Clearinghouse registered a challenge in 1998 from a parent who expressed "concern about the trivialization of sex education." The book was retained.

According to the Colorado Library Research Service there were multiple challenges to Cole's book in Colorado public libraries in 2008. No specifics are provided regarding the challenges, but this book, along with two other picture books, constituted one-third of Colorado challenges in 2008. The Oregon Intellectual Freedom Clearinghouse reported a challenge in 2008 at an unnamed public library. "The parent recommended that the library staff inform patrons about the graphic illustrations and content prior to checking it out."

In 2012 a mother asked that the book be removed from the children's section of the Georgetown, Texas, public library because of "sexual content." She was offended by the illustrations—"clowns in various sexual positions explaining the anatomy." She was informed of the procedure to file a formal challenge

## AWARDS AND ACCOLADES

1994  British Illustrated Children's Book of the Year
*LA Parent Magazine* Award

## AUTHOR'S OFFICIAL WEBSITE

www.babette-cole.com

## FURTHER READING

### Author/Illustrator

www.achuka.co.uk/archive/interviews/babetteint.php. Puffin Books/UK.
www.puffin.co.uk/nf/Author/AuthorPage/0,,1000002483,00.html. Puffin
    Books/UK.

### Censorship

Pohlman, Sara Jane. "Library Book Has Lodia Patty Garcia Worried." *Lodi
    News-Sentinel* (Lodi, California), August 2, 2013. www.lodinews
    .com/news/article_f9671060–655e-5fd3–8bd9–4475dfc09867.html.

### For Listening and Viewing

www.authorstream.com/Presentation/kidsqueen-117992-mummy-laid
    -egg-book-teaching-education-ppt-powerpoint. South Columbia
    University. The Progressive Librarians Guild presents a reading of
    *Mommy Laid an Egg* for the 2011 celebration of Banned Books Week.
www.youtube.com/watch?v = svM05VXOBYw. Accessed December 3,
    2012. This is a video clip from the film (available on DVD) of
    *Mommy Laid an Egg*.

## TALKING WITH READERS ABOUT THE ISSUES

- What is the difference in fact and fiction?
- Explain why the mommy and daddy in the book are so silly.
- Why do the kids think they need to set their parents straight about the facts?
- Why are the mommy and daddy embarrassed by the kids' illustrations and explanation about where babies come from?

## RELATED BOOKS CHALLENGED FOR SIMILAR REASONS

Cole, Joanna. **How You Were Born.** *Illustrated by Margaret Miller. New York: HarperCollins, 1994.*

The book was placed on restricted shelves at the Evergreen School District elementary libraries in Vancouver, Washington, in 1987. This was in accordance with a school board policy to restrict student access to sex education books in elementary school libraries.

*Mayle, Peter.* **Where Did I Come From?** *Illustrated by Arthur Robins (new edition). New York: Kensington, 2000.*

This book was challenged in 1994 at the Washoe County Library System in Reno, Nevada, because "nobody in their right mind would give a book like that to children on their own, except a library."

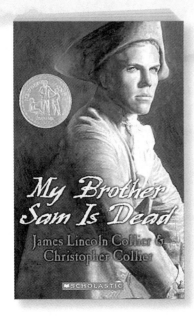

*James Lincoln Collier*
*and Christopher Collier*

# My Brother Sam Is Dead

*New York: Four Winds Press,*
*a division of Scholastic, Inc., 1974*

IT'S 1826, AND TIM MEEKER IS SIXTY-FOUR YEARS OLD WHEN HE RETELLS HIS memories of the American Revolution and how it split his family apart. Sam, his older brother, is a student at Yale when he drops out of school and tells his father that he has enlisted in the Continental Army. Thirteen-year-old Tim is impressed with Sam's uniform and thinks that Sam is courageous and brave. When Sam tells everyone in his father's tavern "it's worth dying to be free," Life Meeker, a Loyalist, cannot control his anger. He sees his son as a traitor who gave up an education for the "wrong" cause. Father and son exchange bitter words and Sam storms out of the tavern in a rage. Tim follows his brother, and Sam confesses that he only came home to get the "Brown Bess," a gun that belongs to his father, to use as a weapon in the war. Sam is so passionate about his beliefs that he tries once again to explain to his father. "Father I am not an Englishman, I am an American, and I am going to fight to keep my country free." His father shouts back, "Get out of my sight. I can't bear to look at you anymore in that vile costume." Sam realizes that he isn't going to convince his father, and leaves his family for the Continental Army.

Tim and his mother think about Sam and worry about his safety, but they understand that they aren't to mention Sam's name to Life Meeker. Tim sees Sam one more time when he comes through town en route to buy cattle for the army. Tim attempts to convince Sam that his family should be more important to him, and he calls Sam a coward. As time goes by,

Tim learns that his father is not so much a Tory as he is against war. But the war is heating up, and it becomes very hard to remain neutral. People in Redding, Pennsylvania, where the Meekers live, believe that everyone is either a Loyalist or a Patriot.

The war has been raging for a while when Tim travels to New York with his father to buy supplies for the tavern. Life Meeker is arrested for selling beef to the British, and eventually dies of cholera on board a prison ship. Tim returns home to become the man of the family. Sam's regiment is camping near Redding, and he slips away to see his mother and brother. He is accused of stealing cattle and is court-martialed and executed a month later.

Tim Meeker wonders "if there might have been another way, beside war, to achieve the same end."

The reviewer for *Kirkus* (September 1, 1974) states, "the uncharacteristically philosophical perspective has impact." *The Bulletin of the Center for Children's Books* (March 1975) says, "Well-paced, the story blends fact and fiction adroitly." The review in the *Christian Science Monitor* (February 26, 1975) states, "Here the paragraphs of an American history book become more than just facts." Though *The Washington Post* (January 12, 1975) raises some issues with the novel, the reviewer says, "Tim's experiences really are enough to make us wonder what we'd have done in his place." The reviewer for the *New York Times Book Review* (November 3, 1974) believes that the book conveys the dilemma that many families faced regarding the war, and says, "The book assumes that children can think."

There are three other books in the series: *The Bloody Country* (1976), *War Comes to Willy Freeman* (1983), and *Who Is Carrie?* (1984).

**CHALLENGES**

The novel was #12 among the 100 Most Frequently Challenged Books: 1990–1999, and #27 in the decade 2000–2009. In 1996 it was #7 on the American Library Association's Top Ten Most Challenged Books. People for the American Way ranked it the 11th Most Challenged book in 1995–1996 and 10th in 1994–1995. There have been challenges for "vulgar and profane language" and "graphic violence" in California, Colorado, Illinois, Kansas, Pennsylvania, South Carolina, and Virginia.

The first recorded challenge to the novel by the Office for Intellectual Freedom was in 1984 in Gwinnett County, Georgia. An abridged version with the profanity deleted was substituted in the elementary school libraries.

The book was removed from the curriculum of fifth-grade classes in New Richmond, Ohio, in 1989 because of "profanity" and it did not represent "acceptable ethical standards for fifth graders." The person bringing the challenge cited the words "bastard," "goddamn," and "hell."

Because the book uses the names of God and Jesus in a "vain and profane manner along with inappropriate sexual references," the book was challenged in the Greenville (South Carolina) school district in 1991.

In 1994 it was removed from fifth-grade classes at Bryant Ranch Elementary School in the Placentia-Yorba Linda (California) Unified School District because "the book is not G-rated. Offensive language is offensive language. Graphic violence is graphic violence, no matter what the context."

"The persistent usage of profanity," as well as references to rape, drinking, and battlefield violence were the reasons for a challenge in 1996 in the Jefferson County Public Schools in Lakewood, Colorado.

A Destin, Florida, minister challenged the novel in 2004, but the Okaloosa School Board voted to retain it.

According to the Texas ACLU Annual Report 2005–2006, the novel was challenged at New Boston Middle School for "drunkenness, gruesome death, and references to alcohol." The book was retained and the student was offered an alternative book.

In 2009 the novel was challenged, but retained in all Muscogee County, Georgia, elementary school libraries, despite a parent's concerns about profanity in the book. It was also challenged in the Rockwell (Texas) Independent School District for "sexual content or nudity and violence or horror." The book was retained in the curriculum, but an alternate book allowed.

Additional challenges reported to the Office for Intellectual Freedom include one in 2012, three in 2009, one in 2006, 2005, 2004, and two in 2003. The institutions reporting the challenges asked to remain anonymous.

## AWARDS AND ACCOLADES

1994 Phoenix Award (Children's Literature Association)
1975 Newbery Honor Book
1975 ALA/ALSC Notable Books for Children
1975 *Horn Book* Fanfare
1975 National Book Award Finalist
1975 Jane Addams Honor Book
1975 ALA/ALSC Notable Children's Book

## FURTHER READING

### The Author

"Christopher Collier," *Contemporary Authors* online, 2001. Books and Authors. Gale.

"James Lincoln Collier," *Contemporary Authors* online, 2010. Books and Authors. Gale.

McElmeel, Sharron L. "Christopher Collier and James Lincoln Collier," *Book Report* 15, no. 2 (September/October 1996): 28–30. www.mcelmeel.com/writing/collier.html.

### The Book

Bickmore, Steven T. "The American Adolescent Historical War Novel: *Johnny Tremain, Rifles for Watie, Across Five Aprils, My Brother Sam Is Dead* as Exemplars." *SIGNAL Journal* 34, no. 1 (Fall 2010/Winter 2011): 19–29.

Collier, Christopher, ed. *Brother Sam and All That: Historical Context and Literary Analysis of the Novels of James and Christopher Collier.* Orange, CT: Clearwater, 1999.

Hurst, Carol O. "Books on the Line." *Teaching Pre K–8* 22, no. 3 (November/December 1991): 112–14.

### Censorship

Collier, Christopher. "Censored: An Author's Perspective." *Censored Books II: Critical Viewpoints 1985–2000,* ed. Nicholas J. Karolides. Lanham, Md.: Scarecrow, 2002, 305–10.

Ryan, Bill. "Politically Correct? Perish the Thought!" *New York Times,* November 5, 1995.

## TALKING WITH READERS ABOUT THE ISSUES

- The novel has been challenged because of "graphic violence." How can there be an accurate depiction of war without violence? What is the most graphic scene in the novel? Rewrite the scene with less violence. How does it change the tone of the book?
- Discuss how the entire Meeker family is affected by the war. How is Tim confused by the conflict between his father and Sam?
- How can war split a family apart? What other American wars have caused families to split loyalties?
- "Profanity and vulgar language" is one of the primary reasons the novel is challenged. How does the language communicate the bitter anger between Sam and his father?
- Some who have brought challenges to the novel are offended by the "sexual references." To what scenes are they referring?
- Some critics call the novel "unpatriotic." Discuss scenes from the novel that cause these critics to make this claim. How might they define patriotism? How would you defend the novel to these critics?

## RELATED BOOKS CHALLENGED FOR SIMILAR REASONS

Anderson, Laurie Halse. **Chains.** *New York: Atheneum, an imprint of Simon and Schuster, 2008.*

According to the Texas ACLU, this novel was challenged in the 2009–2010 school year at Lamkin Elementary School in the Cypress-Fairbanks Independent School District. The reason cited for the challenge was "politically, racially, or socially offensive." It was retained.

Collier, James Lincoln, and Christopher Collier. **War Comes to Willie Freeman.** *New York: Delacorte, a division of Penguin Random House, 1983.*

In 1996, this novel was pulled from two classes at Western Avenue School in Flossmoor, Illinois, after a parent complained that the book "represents totally poor judgment, a complete lack of racial sensitivity and is totally inappropriate for fifth-graders. This book is an education in racism, a primer for developing prejudice."

*Suzanne Collins*

# The Hunger Games

*Scholastic, 2008*

THERE ARE TWELVE DISTRICTS IN PANEM, A post-apocalyptic nation where the Capitol makes all the rules and controls all resources. District 12 is riddled with poverty and that is where sixteen-year-old Katniss Everdeen lives with her mother and younger sister, Prim. After the mining accident that killed her father and devastated the entire District, Katniss's mother suffered an emotional breakdown and is incapable of providing for her daughters. It falls upon Katniss to take over the family. Her best friend is Gale, a boy who lives dangerously by hunting small game in illegal territory. He is the person that teaches Katniss survival skills and how to hunt.

Each year all of Panem anxiously awaits the annual ceremony called the Reaping, where the name of one boy and one girl is drawn to become Tributes, those chosen to fight to the death in a televised battle called The Hunger Games. Prim's name is called, but Katniss cannot allow her little sister to go, and she volunteers to become the girl from District 12. She and Peeta Mellark, a boy from her school, are named the two Tributes, and they leave immediately to begin their training under Haymitch. Katniss knows that the rules allow only one winner, but she has helped Peeta survive to the final showdown, and she must find a way to protect him now. Because of the good training Katniss received from Gale, she develops a scheme to outwit the Capitols. In the camera's eye, she and Peeta fake a love story, and eat poison berries so they both die. When the Capitols turn off the cameras, the two District 12 Tributes spit out the berries, and the Capitols are forced to name two winners of The Hunger Games.

In *Catching Fire* (2009), the second book in the trilogy, Katniss and Peeta are back in District 12 living a comfortable life with their families in the

Victors Village. But President Snow doesn't like to be outwitted, and he is suspicious of the District 12 Tributes. He launches a plan for a second Hunger Games and Katniss and Peeta are once again named. This time Katniss finds herself in uncharted territory when she is deemed an enemy to the Capitol and faces an all-out rebellion that she may have helped create.

The final book is *Mockingjay* (2010). The Districts realize they are the victim of corruption and they launch a rebellion against the Capitol. When they discover that the Capitol is using the Mockingjay as a spy weapon against them, they devise a plan to outwit Capitol and use the Mockingjay to their advantage. Katniss is once again asked to fight, and she must find a way to conquer for her and the society in which she lives. The Capitol is so angry that they destroy District 12. Gale emerges a hero by saving many of the people and escorting them to District 13 where the people there help them.

*Voice of Youth Advocates* (October 1, 2008) calls *The Hunger Games* "a thrilling adventure that will appeal to science fiction, survival, and adventure readers." *School Library Journal* (September 1, 2008) recommends the novel for grades 7–up and states, "Collins's characters are completely realistic and sympathetic as they form alliances and friendships." The reviewer calls the tension in the book "dramatic, and engrossing." In the *Booklist* (September 1, 2008) starred review, Francisca Goldsmith says, "Populated by three-dimensional characters, this is a superb tale of physical adventure, political suspense, and romance." *Publishers Weekly* (November 3, 2008) says, "Readers will wait eagerly to learn more." *Catching Fire* receives praise from reviewers: "Collins explores the complexity of Haymitch, Gale, and the others surrounding Katniss, making them more dimensional," says Deborah L. Dubois in her review in *Voice of Youth Advocates* (December 1, 2009). In the starred review in *Booklist* (July 1, 2009) Ian Chipman writes, "Honestly, this book only needs to be good enough to satisfy its legion of fans. Fortunately, it's great." The reviewer for *School Library Journal* (September 1, 2008) feels that "Katiniss also deepens as a character." *Publishers Weekly* (June 22, 2008) says that the novel "segues into the pulse-pounding action readers have come to expect."

*School Library Journal* (October 1, 2010) calls *Mockingjay* "a fitting end of the series." In the starred review in *Booklist* (September 1, 2010), Ilene Cooper finds the novel hopeful and states, "there is still a human spirit yearning for good." *Publishers Weekly* (August 30, 2010) says that this final book in the trilogy is "the best yet, a beautifully orchestrated and intelligent novel that succeeds on every level."

## CHALLENGES

According to data collected by the ALA's Office for Intellectual Freedom, *The Hunger Games* trilogy was #5 on the Top Ten Most Challenged Books List in 2013, #3 in 2011, and #5 in 2010 because of "graphic depiction of violence, religious viewpoint, and unsuited to age group."

There have also been recorded challenges at the Clover (South Carolina) Middle School and the Walnut Hill School in Shreveport, Louisiana.

In 2010 the trilogy was challenged, but retained at the Mountain View Middle School in Goffstown, New Hampshire. The parent alleged, "lack of morality, violent subject matter that could lead to school violence."

*The Hunger Games* was challenged, but retained at the Kerr Middle School in the Burleson Independent School District in Texas. According to the 2010–2011 Texas ACLU Annual Report, the book was part of the curriculum, and an alternate book was allowed.

There were two challenges cited in the 2012–2013 Texas ACLU Annual Report. The book was part of the curriculum at Bartlett High School in the Bartlett Independent School District and was challenged because the parent felt it "offensive to religious sensitivities." An alternate book was allowed. The trilogy was also challenged, but retained at the Paint Rock School in the Paint Rock Independent School District.

The Mapping Banned Books in Massachusetts's blog, October 25, 2013, reported a challenge in the Dighton Rehoboth Schools. They voted to remove *The Hunger Games* from the elementary school library, but retain it in the middle and high school.

## AWARDS AND ACCOLADES

### The Hunger Games

2012   Georgia Children's Book Award
2012   Nutmeg Children's Book Award: Teen Category (Connecticut)
2011   Black-Eyed Susan Book Award: High School (Maryland)
2011   California Young Reader Medal: Young Adult

2011 Land of Enchantment Book Award: Young Adult (New Mexico)
2011 Garden State Teen Book Award (New Jersey)
2011 Gateway Readers Award (Missouri)
2011 Golden Archer Awards: Middle/Junior High School (Wisconsin)
2011 Grand Canyon Reader Award: Tween Book (Arizona)
2011 Rebecca Caudill Young Reader's Choice Award (Illinois)
2011 Sequoya Book Award: Intermediate and High School (Oklahoma)
2011 South Carolina Book Award: Junior Books and Young Adult Category
2011 Truman Readers Award (Missouri)
2011 Virginia Reader's Choice Award: High School
2011 Young Hoosier Book Award: Middle Books (Indiana)
2010 Blue Hen Book Award: Teen Book (Delaware)
2010 Charlotte Award: Young Adult (New York)
2010 Colorado Blue Spruce Young Adult Book Award
2010 Georgia Peach Book Award for Teen Readers
2010 Pennsylvania Young Reader's Choice Award: Young Adult
2010 Isinglass Teen Read Award (New Hampshire)
2010 Kentucky Bluegrass Award: Grades 9–12
2010 Maine Student Book Award
2010 Rhode Island Teen Book Award
2009 ALA ALSC Notable Childrens' Books: Older Readers
2009 ALA YALSA Best Books for Young Adults
2009 Amelia Bloomer Lists: Young Adult Fiction
2009 Teen Buckeye Award (Ohio)
2009 Thumbs Up Award (Michigan)
2008 *Booklist* Editor's Choice: Books for Youth, Older Readers
2008 *New York Times* Notable Books: Children's Books
2008 *School Library Journal* Best Books

### Catching Fire

2012 Golden Archer Awards: Middle/Junior High School (Wisconsin)
2009 *Booklist* Editor's Choice: Books for Youth, Older Readers

### Mockingjay

2013 Golden Archer Awards: Middle/Junior High School (Wisconsin)
2012 *Booklist* Editor's Choice: Books for Youth, Older Readers

## AUTHOR'S OFFICIAL WEBSITE

www.suzannecollinsbooks.com

## FURTHER READING

### The Author

Hudson, Hannah. "Sit Down with Suzanne Collins." *Instructor* 120 (Fall 2010): 51–53.

Margolis, Rick. "The Last Battle: Interview with Suzanne Collins." *School Library Journal* 56, no. 8 (August 2010): 23–27.

"Suzanne Collins." *Contemporary Authors* online, 2014. Books and Authors. Gale.

### The Book

Gann, Linda A., and Gavigan, Karen. "The Other Side of Dark." *Voice of Youth Advocates* 35, no. 3 (August 2012): 234–38.

Garrow, Hattie. "Don't Be Afraid of the Dark" *Library Media Connection* 31, no. 3 (November/December 2012): 40–41.

Miller, Laura. "Fresh Hell: What's Behind the Boom in Dystopian Fiction for Young Readers." *The New Yorker,* June 14, 2010. www.newyorker .com/arts/critics/atlarge/2010/06/14/100614crat_atlarge_miller.

### Censorship

Hilden, Julie. "A Spate of Complaints Asking Libraries to Censor the *Hunger Games* Trilogy: Why We Should Keep the Books Accessible to Kids." Verdict, April 16, 2012. http://verdict.justia.com/2012/04/ 16/a-spate-of-complaints-asking-libraries-to-censor-the-hunger -games-trilogy.

### For Listening and Viewing

www.youtube.com/watch?v = FH15DI8ZW14. Scholastic, September 2, 2010. In this video, Suzanne Collins speaks about her childhood and the books that she read.

www.youtube.com/watch?v = XEmJJI17rp0 ; www.youtube.com/ watch?v = zUTPQCYVZEQ. *Scholastic,* August 18, 2009. In this two-part video, Suzanne Collins talks about the classical and contemporary inspiration for *The Hunger Games* trilogy.

**TALKING WITH READERS ABOUT THE ISSUES**

- Control and power are underlying themes in the Hunger Games. Discuss the power of those that rule Panem. How do they use their power to control the Districts?
- Discuss why the Hunger Games is televised. Debate whether this is one way the Capitol can maintain control over the people.
- *The Hunger Games* trilogy has been challenged because of the "graphic depiction of violence." Explain how the violence defines the themes of the story.
- The trilogy has also been challenged because of "sexual content." Cite and discuss the sexual scenes. How might you answer someone who claims the books are "sexually explicit"?
- Draw a parallel between the Hunger Games and government corruption. How is this post-apocalyptic trilogy a cautionary story?

**RELATED BOOKS CHALLENGED FOR SIMILAR REASONS**

*Card, Orson Scott.* **Ender's Game.** *New York: Tor Books, 1994.*

A middle school teacher in South Carolina was placed on administrative leave in 2012 when a parent reported him to the police for reading aloud the novel because in her view it's "pornographic." The 2008–2009 Annual Report of the Texas ACLU states that the novel was challenged as part of the curriculum in all junior high schools in the Alvin Independent School District. The book was retained, but an alternate choice was offered students.

*Nelson, O. T.* **The Girl Who Owned the City.** *Minneapolis: Lerner, 1975.*

In 2000 the book was challenged in the Fort Fairfield, Maine, schools because the book promotes violence, including an explanation of how to make a Molotov cocktail.

*Christopher Paul Curtis*

# The Watsons Go to Birmingham—1963

*New York: Delacorte, an imprint of Penguin Random House, 1995*

**SET IN THE 1960S DURING THE CIVIL RIGHTS** Movement, the "Weird Watsons" take a trip from their home in Flint, Michigan, to Birmingham, Alabama, to deliver thirteen-year-old Byron, their oldest son and an "official juvenile delinquent," to his grandmother. Byron is hanging around with the wrong crowd and torments his younger brother, Kenny, a quiet and serious boy who does well in school. Mrs. Watson is much better at dealing with Kenny than she is with Byron. Kenny feels guilty when he hurts his best friend's feelings by joining with the other school kids and laughing at the boy's tattered and torn clothes. Kenny's mother marches her son to the boy's house to apologize. That's all it takes for Kenny. But Byron is a different story. He seems to try hard to do poorly in school, and the thought of dealing with his behavior all summer is more than the Watsons can fathom.

Racial riots are occurring all over Alabama, and the Jim Crow laws throughout the South make it impossible for the Watsons to spend the night in a motel, or even be served a meal in a restaurant. They pack plenty of food and sleep in the car. Two things happen when they get to Birmingham that changes the reason for their trip. Kenny ignores a no-swimming sign, almost drowns, and is saved by Byron. Kenny is surprised when Byron breaks down in sobs. Then the riots of the Civil Rights Movement come right into Grandma Sands's neighborhood and the Sixteenth Street Baptist Church is bombed, killing four young girls. The Watsons fear that Joetta, their youngest child, is in the church. She is safe, but Mr. and Mrs. Watson pack up their three children that very night and head back to Michigan.

Kenny is the one who suffers the most. He isn't interested in seeing friends, and he spends days and nights behind the sofa. Byron becomes a caring brother and sleeps on the couch so that Kenny won't be alone. Finally, in a tender scene at the end of the novel, Byron tells Kenny, "There ain't nothing wrong with being sad or scared about that. I'm sad about it too. I got real scared." As horrible as the Birmingham trip was for the Watsons, they returned home a different family—Byron included.

Hazel Rochman, reviewer for *Booklist* (August 1995), says, "In this compelling first novel, form and content are one." *School Library Journal* (October 1, 1995) states that the novel is "a totally believable child's view of the world." *Publishers Weekly* (October 1995) gives the novel a starred review and calls it "an exceptional first novel." *Kirkus* (October 1, 1995) says the narrator has a "distinct, believable voice." *Voice of Youth Advocates* (December 1, 1995) calls the novel "a touching and powerful story." Martha V. Paravano, reviewer for *Horn Book Magazine* (March/April 1996), states, "Curtis's control of his material is superb."

## CHALLENGES

In 1995 the Texas ACLU recorded the first known challenge to the novel. A parent filed a challenge with the Alamo Heights School District because of "violence."

In 1998 there was a challenge in Wisconsin, but the institution filing the challenge with the Office for Intellectual Freedom asked that the details of the complaint remain "private."

In 2002 the novel was challenged in the Stafford County (Virginia) middle schools because of "offensive language."

A challenge was filed with ALA's Office for Intellectual Freedom in 2005 for "racism, political view," and "offensive language." The library asked to remain anonymous.

## AWARDS AND ACCOLADES

2000  Land of Enchantment Book Award: Young Adult (New Mexico)
1998  California Young Readers Award
1996  Newbery Honor Book
1996  Coretta Scott King Honor Book

1996   ALA/ALSC Notable Children's Book
1996   ALA/YALSA Best Books
1996   Golden Kite Award for Fiction
1995   ALA Top Ten Best Books/Quick Picks
1995   Josette Frank Award

## AUTHOR'S OFFICIAL WEBSITE

www.nobodybutcurtis.com

## PUBLISHER'S OFFICIAL WEBSITE

www.randomhouse.com/features/christopherpaulcurtis

## FURTHER READING

### The Author

"Christopher Paul Curtis." *Contemporary Authors* online, 2008. Books and
    Authors. Gale.
Curtis, Christopher Paul. "Drawing Back the Curtain: Momma's Inspira-
    tion. . . . and The Making of a Writer." *Children and Libraries: The
    Journal of the Association for Library Service to Children* 7 (Summer
    2009): 21–28.
Parker-Rock, Michelle. *Christopher Paul Curtis: An Author Kids Love.*
    Berkeley Heights, NJ: Enslow, 2009. 48 p. (Authors Kids Love Series)
Rochman, Hazel. "Christopher Paul Curtis." *Booklist* 104 (February 1,
    2008): 54.
Schneider, Dean. "Talking with Christopher Paul Curtis." *Book Links,* a
    publication of *Booklist* 18, no. 2 (November 2008): 14–16.
www.nypl.org/author-chat-christopher-paul-curtis. Transcript of a live
    chat by the New York Public Library, August 7, 2002.

### The Book

*All Things Considered.* "'Birmingham': A Family Tale in the Civil Rights
    Era." Transcript. January 26, 2012. www.npr.org/2012/01/26/
    145718692/a-teenagers-take-on-the-civil-rights-movement.

Chaudhri, Amina. "'Straighten Up and Fly Right': Hetero Masculinity in *The Watsons Go to Birmingham—1963.*" *Children's Literature Association Quarterly* 36, no. 2 (Summer 2011): 147–63.

Curtis, Christopher Paul. "*The Watsons Go to Birmingham—1963*" (cover story). *Scholastic Scope* 53 (January 10, 2005): 16–18.

McNair, Jonda C. "'I May Be Crackin,' But Um Fackin': Racial Humor in *The Watsons Go to Birmingham—1963.*" *Children's Literature in Education* 39, no. 3 (September 2008): 201–12.

Paul, Daniel. "Appointment with History." *Writing* 26 (February/March 2004): 20–23.

**For Listening and Viewing**

www.youtube.com/watch?v = r8Y8I9x6UEY. AdLit.org, January 19, 2011. Christopher Paul Curtis talks about his life and becoming a writer.

http://arts.gov/search/content/Christopher%20Paul%20Curtis. Podcast and transcript provided by the National Endowment for the Arts, August 23, 2012. Christopher Paul Curtis allows readers and listeners into his life as a writer.

www.readingrockets.org/books/interviews/curtis. *Reading Rockets,* April 25, 2011. This video interview with Christopher Paul Curtis for *Reading Rockets* is also available on YouTube.

## TALKING WITH READERS ABOUT THE ISSUES

- Discuss the Jim Crow laws in the South in the 1960s when the "Weird Watsons" travel to Birmingham, Alabama. Kenny and Byron have never been victims of such laws. Discuss their reaction as the Watsons officially cross over into the South.
- Even with all the trouble brewing in the South, Mrs. Watson still misses things about living in Birmingham. How does she compare racism in Michigan to that in Alabama?
- The bombing of the Sixteenth Baptist Church is a tragedy that the Watsons may never forget. How does Kenny deal with the bombing emotionally?
- How does the bombing change Byron? Explain how he becomes a better brother. Discuss whether this change is likely to stay with him.

- Explain how knowing about the Civil Rights Movement is important. What are the important lessons to take from the era?

## RELATED BOOKS CHALLENGED FOR SIMILAR REASONS

*Grove, Vicki,* **The Starplace.** *New York: Putnam, an imprint of Penguin Random House, 1999.*

In 2008 this novel was challenged at the Turner Elementary School in New Tampa, Florida, because it contains a "racial epithet." The book is about an interracial middle-school friendship in 1960s Oklahoma and was highly recommended by *Children's Literature Review*.

*Taylor, Mildred D.* **Mississippi Bridge.** *New York: Dial, an imprint of Penguin Random House, 1990.*

In 2001 this book was challenged, but retained at the Donahoe Elementary School Library in Sandston, Virginia, despite objections to its "negative content and (that) it's riddled with prejudice."

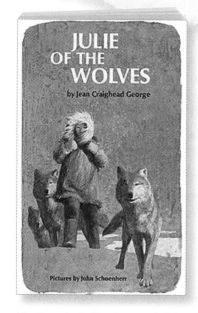

*Jean Craighead George*

# Julie of the Wolves

*New York: Harper and Row*
*(now HarperCollins), 1972*

**MIYAX, WHOSE AMERICAN NAME IS JULIE,** was only four years old when Kapugen, her widowed father, left her with Aunt Martha in the village of Mekoryuk, Alaska, and disappeared from her life. Before he left, Kapugen made an agreement with Naka, an Eskimo who practices "old-time" traditions, that when Miyax turned thirteen she would marry his son, Daniel. In June of her thirteenth year Miyax receives word from the head of Indian Affairs that she is to go to Daniel. Aunt Martha explains that Miyax may refuse the arrangement, but Miyax feels that she must keep her father's promise. She flies to Barrow, Alaska, where she meets Daniel for the first time. Miyax notices that Daniel's eyes are dull, and feels that something is very wrong with him. His mother admits that Daniel has problems, and says, "He will be like a brother to you."

Miyax doesn't mind the idea of a brother, but to her surprise there is a wedding planned for the next day. Unhappy and confused, she desperately wants a letter from her pen pal in San Francisco and dreams of becoming "Julie" and adopting an American way of life. Pearl Norman, a married girl Miyax's age, assures her, "All you have to do is leave the house or run away and everything's forgotten. Most of these arrangements are for convenience." Things get worse for Miyax when Daniel comes home in a rage and commits marital rape. This encounter with Daniel finally gives Miyax the courage to escape "her Eskimo culture" and begin the search for a new place to live.

In her journey to find a new home, Miyax becomes lost on the Alaskan tundra and discovers that the only way she can survive is to become friends with a pack of Arctic wolves. After days on the tundra, she comes upon a hunter and his wife who lead her to Kangik, and to her surprise, she finds Kapugen and his Caucasian wife. She is astonished to discover that her father, the same man who practiced the "old ways" and arranged for her to marry Daniel, now lives with modern conveniences and hunts from an airplane that he owns.

In *Julie* (1994), Miyax pledges to save the wolves from hunters like Kapugen. *Julie's Wolf Pack* (1997) takes readers back to the tundra, where the story continues—from the wolves' point of view.

*Kirkus* (November 1, 1972) states, "Miyax and her experience are totally believable." *The Bulletin of the Center for Children's Books* (March 1973) called the novel "taut in structure, poignant in implication." The reviewer for *Booklist* (February 1, 1973) says, "the well-written, empathetic story effectively evokes the nature of wolves and the traditional Eskimo way of life." And the *Horn Book* (February 1973) reviewer states the books has elements of "classic dimensions."

" I'm delighted to be on the list of Banned Books. To think that I am in the company of Mark Twain, the Bible, and other giants of literature is mind blowing. What an esteemed group."

—Jean Craighead George, author of *Julie of the Wolves*

## CHALLENGES

According to the ALA's Office for Intellectual Freedom, this novel was #10 on the Top Ten Most Challenged List in 2002 because it was deemed "unsuited to age group and violence." It was also #38 on the 100 Most Challenged Books List: 1990–2000.

In 1982 the novel was challenged, but retained in Mexico, Missouri, because of the "socialist, communist, evolutionary and anti-family themes."

A sixth-grade classroom in Littleton, Colorado, was the target of a challenge in 1994. The challenge cited "alcoholism, abuse, and divorce" as reasons for the complaint. The book was retained. In the same year, it was challenged at Erie Elementary School in Chandler, Arizona, because of the "sexual assault" scene. The book was removed from the shelves.

Parents of a student in the Palmdale School District in southern California requested that the novel be removed because of the "sexual assault" scene. Although the book had been reviewed by a committee before it was used with students, the materials review committee thought the book more appropriate for older readers.

In 1996 the book was removed from the sixth-grade curriculum of the New Brighton Area School District in Pulaski, Pennsylvania, because of the "graphic rape scene." It was also challenged at the Hanson Lane Elementary School in Ramona, California, for the same reason.

The book was challenged in the school curriculum in Arizona and Maine in 2002. The parent who brought the challenge in Arizona was concerned about the "violence." The person who challenged the book in Maine simply stated that it was "unsuited for age group." The schools involved in these challenges asked to remain anonymous, and the status of the challenges is unknown. In the same year, a challenge at a public library in Texas was reported and cited "unsuited for age group." The book was retained.

In 2006 California schools were informed that the state standards recommended *Julie of the Wolves* for grades 6–8.

In 2011 the novel was challenged in the school curriculum in New Jersey because of "violence, sexually explicit and unsuited for age group." The status is unknown.

A challenge was reported in 2013 in a school library in North Carolina. The person who issued the challenge felt that the novel was "sexually explicit and unsuited for age group." According to the North Carolina School Library Media Association, the book was retained.

## AWARDS AND ACCOLADES

1976   *Julie of the Wolves:* Ten Best Children's Books in 200 Years: Children's Literature Association
1973   John Newbery Medal
1973   National Book Award Finalist

## AUTHOR'S OFFICIAL WEBSITE

www.jeancraigheadgeorge.com

Jean Craighead George is deceased, but the website will continue to be updated.

## FURTHER READING

### The Author

"Author Chat with Jean Craighead George," a transcript of a live interview at the New York Public Library. August 17, 2004. www.nypl .org/author-chat-jean-craighead-george.

Bader, Barbara. "Jean of the Wolves." *Horn Book Magazine* 85, no. 1 (January/February 2009): 43. http://archive.hbook.com/magazine/ articles/2009/jan09_bader.asp.

Ellas, Tana. "Jean Craighead George and the Natural World: An Interview with Jean Craighead George." *Friends of the CCBC Newsletter,* 2000. https://ccbc.education.wisc.edu/authors/experts/george.asp.

Hopkins, Lee Bennett. "Jean Craighead George." *Elementary English* 50 (October 1973): 1049–53.

Hopkinson, Deborah. "Jean Craighead George: A Nature Loving Author Searches for Paradise in the Swamp." *BookPage* (May 2002). http://bookpage.com/interviews/8141-jean-craighead-george# .Uy8Ap9xOF4M.

### The Book

George, Jean Craighead. "Newbery Acceptance Speech." *Horn Book Magazine* 49 (August 1973): 337–47.

Kuznets, Lois R. "The Female Pastoral Journey in *Julie of the Wolves* and *A Wild Thing.*" In *Webs and Wardrobes: Humanist and Religious World Views in Children's Literature,* ed. Joseph O'Beirne Milner and Lucy Floyd Morcock Milner, 99–110. Lanham, MD: University Press of America, 1987.

Lickteig, Mary. "*Julie of the Wolves* and *Dogsong:* The Cultural Conflict between the Inuits and the Dominant American Culture." In *Cross-Culturalism in Children's Literature: Selected Papers from the 1987 International Conference of the Children's Literature Association,* ed. Susan R. Gannon and Ruth Anne Thompson, 83–86. Toronto: Pace University, 1987.

Report in *Children's Literature Review*. Ed. Tom Burns. Vol. 136. Detroit: Gale. From Literature Resource Center.

Report in *Children's Literature Review*. Ed. Scot Peacock. Vol. 82. Detroit: Gale, 2003. From Literature Resource Center.

**Censorship**

George, Jean Craighead. "Challenged Books, Blurred Boundaries." *Newsletter on Intellectual Freedom* 40 (November 1997): 191.

**For Listening and Viewing**

www.youtube.com/watch?v = oNF0WF9DF5U. OpenRoadMedia Videos, August 31, 2011. Jean Craighead George talks about her life as a naturalist and writer.

www.youtube.com/watch?v = OC_40QJmZSA. ALA/OIF, October 19, 2012. Wendell Minor, illustrator, reads from *Julie of the Wolves* for Banned Books Week.

## TALKING WITH READERS ABOUT THE ISSUES

- Aunt Martha tells Miyax that she can refuse the marriage arrangement that Kapugen made for her. Why does Miyax feel she must honor her father's promise?
- How is Julie caught between two cultures? Trace the theme of survival in the three parts of the book.
- *Julie of the Wolves* has been challenged in many schools because Daniel, after being teased by some boys, enters the house in a rage and tries to "mate" with Miyax. Discuss whether Daniel means to hurt her. How does Daniel's "slow mentality" contribute to the way the scene plays out?
- Jean Craighead George once said that she didn't view this scene as "rape," and was surprised when the novel was censored for "sexual content" and "violence." How do you view the scene?
- Discuss whether this "alleged rape" scene is too violent for young readers. How is the book about so much more than this one scene?

## RELATED BOOKS CHALLENGED FOR SIMILAR REASONS

*Clauser, Suzanne.* **A Girl Named Sooner.** *Discus Books, 1999.*

In 1999, this novel was removed from the Jefferson Middle School in Oregon because of "its explicit sexual content."

*Cushman, Karen.* **The Midwife's Apprentice.** *Boston: Harcourt Houghton Mifflin, 1995.*

The Texas ACLU recorded a challenge to this 1996 John Newbery Medal winner at Coldspring Elementary School in the Coldspring Independent School District in 2007 because of "sexual content." There is a reference to "a roll in the hay."

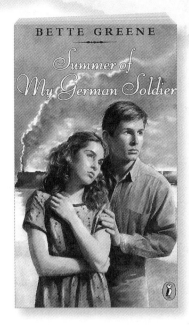

*Bette Greene*

# Summer of My German Soldier

*New York: Dial, an imprint of Penguin Random House, 1973; New York: Puffin, an imprint of Penguin Random House, 1999; New York: Open Road Media (e-book), 2011*

SET DURING WORLD WAR II IN THE SMALL TOWN OF JENKINSVILLE, ARKANSAS, twelve-year-old Patty Bergen is the oldest child of the only Jewish family in town. Most of the people in Jenkinsville already harbor racial and ethnic prejudices, but these bigotries turn into apprehension the summer the U.S. government sets up a German POW camp just outside of town. Patty doesn't have many friends in this "all Christian" town, but even the girls in her class at school are away for the summer. She is lonely and at loose ends. Her parents dote on her younger sister, and Patty is the victim of their wrath—abusive screaming and even beatings by her dad while her mother sits idly by. Only Ruth, the black housekeeper, sees Patty's worth.

When the German POWs are brought into Mr. Bergen's store to purchase hats, Patty strikes up a brief conversation with one of them. Then there is news that a German soldier has escaped. Patty spots him on their property, recognizes him as the soldier she spoke with in the store, and provides him with a hiding place. Anton gives her a special ring from his finger and Patty wears it around her neck. The FBI is called in and Patty is the one interrogated. It is the ring that implicates her. Patty is too young to be tried for treason, but she is sent to reformatory school for several months where her only visitor is Ruth. Patty knows that she has disgraced her family, but she also knows that they have never loved her the way a daughter should be loved. The need to belong, and to be loved are central themes in the novel. During the summer of her German soldier, it never really occurred to Patty that she was a Jewish girl hiding a Nazi. She only cared that he gave her attention.

*Morning Is a Long Time Coming* (1978) is a sequel, and begins when Patty is eighteen and goes to Europe in search of Anton's family.

*The New York Times Book Review* (November 4, 1973) calls the novel "an exceptionally fine novel." *Horn Book Magazine* (February 1974) calls it "unforgettable because of the genuine emotion it evokes." Jane Abramson, reviewer for *School Library Journal* (October 15, 1973), doesn't think the novel works, and calls it "a far-fetched and flummoxed first novel."

## CHALLENGES

The novel was #55 on the American Library Association's Top 100 Banned/ Challenged Books list 2000–2009 because of "offensive language, racism, and sexually explicit. " It was #88 on the 1990–1999 100 Most Frequently Challenged Books.

1990 is the earliest challenge recorded by the ALA's Office for Intellectual Freedom. That challenge was in Burlington, Connecticut, schools because the book contains "profanity and subject matter that set bad examples and gives students negative views of life."

There was another challenge in Connecticut in 1996. This time it was in the Hawinton schools for the same reasons as the challenge in Burlington.

In 1996 the novel was temporarily removed from an eighth-grade supplemental reading list in Cinnaminson, New Jersey, because it contains "offensive racial stereotypes."

## AWARDS AND ACCOLADES

1980  Massachusetts Children's Book Award
1974  ALA/ALSC Notable Children's Books
1974  Golden Kite Author Award
1973  National Book Award Nominee
1973  *New York Times* Outstanding Book Award
1973  National Book Award Nominee

## AUTHOR'S OFFICIAL WEBSITE

www.bettegreene.com

## FURTHER READING

### The Author

"Bette Greene." *Contemporary Authors* online, 2006. Books and Authors. Gale.

Bette Evensky Greene. *Encyclopedia of Arkansas History and Culture.* www.encyclopediaofarkansas.net/encyclopedia/entry-detail .aspx?entryID=1035.

### The Book

Benoit, Rosalie. "Bette Greene's *Summer of My German Soldier*: The War within the Human Heart." In *Censored Books II: Critical Viewpoints, 1985–2000.* Lanham, MD: Scarecrow, 2002.

Hagen, Lyman. "Summer of My German Soldier." In *Beacham's Guide to Literature for Young Adults,* ed. Kirk H. Beetz and Suzanne Niemeyer. Vol. 3, pp. 1298–1303. Washington, DC: Beacham, 1990.

Osa, Osayimwense. "Adolescent Girls' Need for Love in Two Cultures: Nigeria and the United States." *English Journal* 72, no. 8 (December 1983): 35–37.

Report in *Children's Literature Review.* Ed. Tom Burns. Vol. 40. Detroit: Gale, 2009. From Literature Resource Center.

### Censorship

Greene, Bette. "An Author's Perspective on Censorship and Selection." *Library Talk* 14, no. 2 (March/April 2001): 12–14.

Report in *Children's Literature Review.* Ed. Tom Burns. Vol. 40 Detroit: Gale, 2009. From Literature Resource Center.

### For Listening and Viewing

www.youtube.com/watch?v=XTcPMjI57dU. OpenRoadMedia Videos, October 2011. Bette Greene talks about the true story that was the inspiration for *Summer of My German Soldier.*

## TALKING WITH READERS ABOUT THE ISSUES

- Discuss the prejudices that exist in Jenkinsville. How are these related to the era?
- Describe what it's like for Patty Bergen, the only Jewish girl in town.
- The German POWs are brought into Patty's father's store. Discuss Patty's first reaction to them. How does her attitude change when the one named Anton speaks to her?
- Debate whether the verbal and physical abuse that Patty suffers from her parents contributes to her willingness to hide Anton.
- Describe Patty's relationship with Ruth. How does Ruth understand Patty in ways that her parents never will? Discuss how Mr. Bergen treats Ruth when she defends Patty. How are his prejudices against Ruth similar to the prejudices his family is victim of in the "all-Christian" town?

## RELATED NOVELS CHALLENGED FOR SIMILAR REASONS

*Kerr, M. E.* **Gentlehands.** *New York: HarperCollins, 1978.*

In 1983 the novel was challenged at the Lake Braddock Secondary School in Virginia because it was considered "anti-Semitic."

*Reiss, Johanna.* **The Upstairs Room.** *New York: Thomas Y. Crowell, an imprint of HarperCollins, 1972 (new edition, 1987).*

In 1996, this 1973 Newbery Honor Book was challenged as assigned reading for sixth-grade students in Sanford, Maine, because of "profanity." It was removed from the required reading list for fourth-graders at Liberty Elementary School in Indiana in 1993.

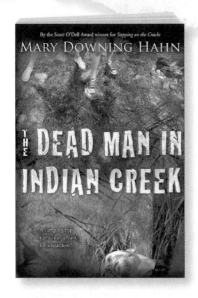

*Mary Downing Hahn*

## Dead Man in Indian Creek

*Boston: Houghton Mifflin Harcourt Publishing Co., 1990*

MATTHEW ARMENTROUT AND PARKER PET-
tengill are in junior high school when they
go on a camping trip and discover a dead man in Indian Creek. Parker sees
George Evans, the owner of a local antique store and his mother's boss and
boyfriend, standing at the top of a bridge. The boys take their information
to the police, but are quickly dismissed as having a wild and vivid imagination. Parker's suspicions grow and he convinces Matt to help him spy on
the antique store. On Halloween night they stake out the store and make
a startling discovery. George Evans is indeed involved and so is Parker's
mother, Pam. They are stuffing cocaine in the heads of antique dolls and
turning them over to drug dealers. The boys devise a plan to get one of the
dolls to the police. This time the boys become local heroes for exposing a
drug ring in their quiet town of Woodcroft. When George wrecks his van
in a getaway, Pam lands in the hospital with a broken leg. Parker is devastated that his mother is involved, but is assured by Matt that they probably
saved Pam from suffering a similar fate as the dead man in Indian Creek.

*The Bulletin of the Center for Children's Books* (April, 1990) recommends
the novel for grades 5–8 and says that Hahn has "an exceptional command
of suspenseful pacing." Ilene Cooper, reviewer for *Booklist* (February 15,
1990), recommends the book for grades 6–8 and states, "what sets the book
apart are Hahn's insightful character sketches, especially her portrayal of
Matt, whose first-person musings will both entertain and give pause." The
reviewer for *Publishers Weekly* (February 9, 1990) says, "A combination of
crackling language and plenty of suspense, this fast-paced yarn is likely to

appeal to even the most reluctant readers." They recommend the novel for ages 9–13. Carolyn Noah, the reviewer for *School Library Journal* (April 1, 1990), recognizes that the novel is filled with suspense and states, "Hahn's effortless mastery of kids' dialogue makes this an easy read."

## CHALLENGES

In 1994 the novel was challenged in the Salem-Keizer (Oregon) School District elementary schools because of "graphic violence and examples of inappropriate parenting."

In 2007 the Texas ACLU recorded a challenge and ultimate ban of the novel at Monahan Elementary School in the Sheldon Independent School District, Houston, because of "explicit references to drug and alcohol use. " The complainant took issue with the mother smuggling drugs as a way of dealing with financial difficulties.

The novel was challenged in 2010 at the Salem-Keizer (Oregon) School District elementary schools for "drugs and drug smuggling activities."

## AWARDS AND ACCOLADES

1994  Virginia Young Reader's Award
1993  Beehive Award (Utah)
1993  Indian Young Hoosier Award
1993  Iowa Children's Choice Award
1993  Maud Hart Lovelace Book Award
1993  South Carolina Children's Book Award
1993  Utah Children's Choice Award
1991  International Reading Association/Children's Book Council Children's Choices
1990  American Library Association Quick Picks for Young Adult Readers

## AUTHOR'S OFFICIAL WEBSITE

www.hmhbooks.com/features/mdh

## FURTHER READING

### The Author

"Mary Downing Hahn." The Children's Book Guild of Washington DC.
www.childrensbookguild.org/mary-downing-hahn.

"Mary Downing Hahn." *Contemporary Authors* online, 2013. Books and
Authors. Gale.

McMahon, Judith. "A Visit with Mary Downing Hahn." *School Library
Journal* 40 (August 1994): 75–76.

Miller, Doug. "Mary Downing Hahn." *Howard County Times* (Columbia,
MD), March 11, 2010.

Sutton, Roger. "Mary Downing Hahn Talks with Roger." *Horn Book
Magazine* (June 2, 2012). www.hbook.com/2012/06/talks-with
-roger/mary-downing-hahn-talks-with-roger.

### For Listening and Viewing

www.fcps.edu/fairfaxnetwork/mta/hahn.html. Fairfax County, Virginia,
Public Schools. A student interviews Mary Downing Hahn.

## TALKING WITH READERS ABOUT THE ISSUES

- How might Parker describe Pam as a mother?
- Why is Parker so convinced that George Evans is guilty of a crime?
- Debate whether Parker and Matthew acted responsibly when they
  staked out the antique shop on Halloween night.
- Describe Parker's reaction when he discovers that his mother is
  guilty.
- What is an appropriate response to adults who believe that children
  shouldn't read about drug-related crimes, or about parents who
  aren't good role models?

## RELATED BOOKS CHALLENGED FOR SIMILAR REASONS

*Cooney, Caroline B.* **The Face on the Milk Carton.** *New York: Delacorte, an imprint of Penguin Random House, 1996.*

This title was #80 on the American Library Association's 100 Most Challenged Books: 1990–1999, and rose to #29 in the decade 2000–2009 because the main character challenges authority when she takes matters in her own hands to uncover the mystery of her true identity and how her parents are involved in the cover-up. The novel was also challenged in the Flour Bluff (Texas) Independent School District in the school year 2002–2003.

*Ewing, Lynne.* **Drive-By.** *New York: HarperCollins, 1997.*

A parent challenged this novel at the middle school Library in Bleyl, Texas, in the 2002–2003 school year because of "violence related to death and drug money."

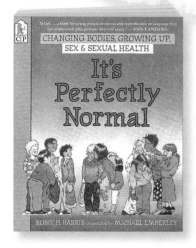

*Robie H. Harris*

# It's Perfectly Normal: A Book about Changing Bodies, Growing Up, Sex, and Sexual Health

*Illustrated by Michael Emberley. Cambridge: Candlewick, 1994*
*(15th anniversary edition, 2009)*

ROBIE HARRIS SAYS THAT "HAVING QUESTIONS IS NORMAL," AND SHE OFFERS pre-adolescent readers the answers to their most burning questions about sex and sexuality, and their changing bodies. The information is candid, and the illustrations offer a visual interpretation of each topic. There is discussion about sexual intercourse, and the illustrations do reveal what that looks like, but that isn't all the book is about. A discussion about what it means to be a sexual being, the changes that bodies undergo during puberty, and the importance of sexual health are all part of the text. The illustrations make no mystery out of the developing male and female body. Homosexuality is discussed, as is safe sex. There is information about AIDS and sexually transmitted diseases that threaten the health of heterosexuals and homosexuals.

Emberley's cartoon style allows him to convey information clearly and accurately, without a biology or health textbook feel. Some of the illustrations are humorous, such as the panels that show eggs traveling through the Fallopian tubes into the uterus ("Wheeee!! That was fun!"). Numerous illustrations show naked bodies in various situations and from many angles. Throughout, two cartoon characters, a bird and a bee, comment on the information presented.

The starred review in *Kirkus* (September 15, 1994) calls the book "a terrific teaching tool." *Horn Book Magazine* (March 1, 1995) says the book is a "comprehensive explanation of sex." *Booklist* (September 15, 1994) recommends the book for grades 4–7 and says that the forthright text and illustrations make it a "marvelous adjunct to the middle-school sex-education curriculum." *Publishers Weekly* (July 18, 1994) gives the book a star and praises the "conversational, relaxed tone" of both the text and illustrations. And *School Library Journal* (December 1, 1994) says that it is "frank yet playful."

" I would never, ever say that my books should be in every home, every school, or every library or bookstore in America. But I would say that in our democracy, any person, any family, school, library, organization, health professional, or clergy member who chooses to have my books should have the right to do so and that right needs to be respected and protected as well."

—Robie Harris, author of *It's Perfectly Normal: A Book about Changing Bodies, Growing Up, Sex, and Sexual Health*

## CHALLENGES

This book was #1 on the American Library Association's Most Challenged List in 2005, #7 in 2003, and #9 in 2007.

In 2001, a parent challenged the book because of "value statements" and because "marriage is mentioned once in the whole book, while homosexual relationships are allocated an entire section," which caused the Anchorage (Alaska) School District to restrict the book to pupils with parental permission.

In 2003 the book was relocated from the young adult to the adult section of the Fort Bend County Public Libraries in Richmond, Texas. The same title was moved to the restricted section of the Fort Bend School District's libraries after a resident sent an e-mail message to the superintendent expressing concern about the book's content. The Spirit of Freedom Republican Women's Club petitioned the superintendent to have it, along with *It's So Amazing,* moved because they contain "frontal nudity and discussion of homosexual relationships and abortion."

An Auburn Public Library patron in Lewiston, Maine, challenged the book in 2007 because she was "sufficiently horrified by the illustrations and sexually graphic, amoral, abnormal contents."

In 2011 the book was challenged, but retained at Lee County, Florida, libraries despite the book's explicit illustrations.

## AWARDS AND ACCOLADES

1995 ALA/ALSC Notable Children's Books List
1995 *New York Times* Best Book of the Year
1994 *Booklist* Editors' Choice: Books for Youth
1994 *Publishers Weekly* Best Book of the Year
1994 New York Public Library "Top 100 Titles of the Year"
1994 *School Library Journal* Best Books List
1994 *Wilson Library Bulletin* Favorite Reads

## AUTHOR'S OFFICIAL WEBSITE

http://robieharris.com

## ILLUSTRATOR'S OFFICIAL WEBSITE

www.michaelemberley.com

## FURTHER READING

### The Author

Ellas, Tana. "The Perfectly Amazing Robie Harris: An Interview with Robie Harris." *Friends of the CCBC Newsletter* (2000). http://ccbc .education.wisc.edu/authors/experts/harris.asp.

"Robie H. Harris." *Contemporary Authors* online, 2010. Books and Authors. Gale.

Zvirin, Stephanie. "Interview: Robie Harris." *Booklist* 92 (May 1, 1996): 1495.

### The Book

Allen, Sara. "Sex Talks: Out Loud and Proud." *The Oregonian* (Portland, OR), June 10, 2001.

Bringelson, Carin, and Nick Glass. "Presenting Human Development and Sexuality to Children and Teens." *School Library Monthly* 26 (May 2010): 27.

Harris, Robie H. "It's Perfectly Normal in the Age of the Internet." *Advocates for Youth.* www.advocatesforyouth.org/parents/1526 ?task = view.

LaPiana, Maria. "An Open Book—'It's Perfectly Normal' Takes a Candid Look at Sex and Good Sense." *Sacramento Bee* (California), November 12, 1994.

## Censorship

Crispin, Jessa. "Robie H. Harris on Life on the Banned Books List." *Kirkus* (September 25, 2012). https://www.kirkusreviews.com/features/ robie-h-harris-challenges-banned-books.

Harris, Robie H. "Censorship of the Written Word: Still Alive and Kickin.'" *Newsletter on Intellectual Freedom* 53 (September 2004): 168–206.

Harris, Robie H. "Robie Harris on the Banning of Her Books." *Pen America/Free Expression Literature,* October 15, 2012. www.pen.org/ nonfiction/robie-harris-banning-her-books.

## For Listening and Viewing

www.youtube.com/watch?v = KanTCR-1EuI. September 1, 2012. Robie H. Harris talks about giving the parents the tools to talk about the birds and the bees with children.

www.teachingbooks.net/author_collection.cgi?id = 16&a = .
Michael Emberley demonstrates his art technique and style.

## TALKING WITH READERS ABOUT THE ISSUES

- Discuss why locker room talk about sex is often the wrong information. How do you know when you have the right information?
- How does reading an informational book about sex and growing up feel more private than asking an adult for answers? Discuss how books may help you form questions you would like to ask.
- *It's Perfectly Normal* has been banned in some schools and libraries because of the illustrations. How do the illustrations combine with the text to provide accurate information?

- Other critics feel that the book promotes homosexuality. Why is it important to include information about homosexuality in a book like *It's Perfectly Normal*?
- There is a tendency to laugh when a discussion becomes uncomfortable. Discuss why sex should be no laughing matter among young adolescents. Explain why information about sex helps adolescents stay "healthy and safe."

## RELATED BOOKS CHALLENGED FOR SIMILAR REASONS

*Bailey, Jacqui, and Jan McCafferty.* **Sex, Puberty, and All That Stuff: A Guide to Growing Up.** *Hauppague, NY: Barron's Educational Series, 2004.*

This book was retained in the Windsor Connecticut Library in 2008 after being challenged as inappropriate for its descriptions of sexual development.

*Cole, Joanna.* **Asking about Sex and Growing Up.** *New York: HarperCollins, 2009 (revised edition)*

In 1994, this book was challenged, but retained in the Anchorage (Alaska) School District elementary school libraries despite complaints that it is "inappropriate for elementary school children and teaches values opposed to those of the majority of parents."

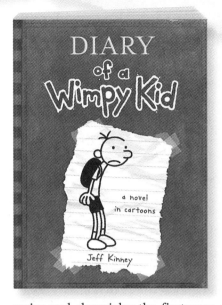

*Jeff Kinney*

## Diary of a Wimpy Kid series

*New York: Amulet Books,
an imprint of Abrams, 2007–present*

**DIARY OF A WIMPY KID: GREG HEFFLEY'S** *Journal* (2007) is the first book in the series and chronicles the first year of middle school for Greg Heffley. The diary was his mother's idea, so Greg writes every day, leaving nothing out. And he draws little figures within the text that communicate exactly what he is feeling. He records what it feels like to be an undersized kid sandwiched between more mature boys, some who even need to shave. He describes the usual middle-school struggles: girls, pranks, bullies, and friends. All of these things are tough, but he finds himself at loose ends when he and his best friend, Rowley, an original wimp, drift apart. Rowley has climbed the sixth-grade "popularity" ladder, which means that Greg must resort to desperate measures to win back his friend. Greg is about to start a new school year in *Rodrick Rules* (2008) and he is worried that his older brother, Rodrick, will expose the secret summer incident that could possibly ruin him. Greg thinks this might be the year to impress the girls, and the secret incident could cause him to fail. The third book in the series, *The Last Straw* (2009), is a battle between father and son. When his father vows to send him to military school if he doesn't change his "wimpy" ways, Greg searches for ways to dodge the threat while dealing with a new set of middle-school challenges. In *Dog Days* (2009), the Heffley family is stuck with one another for the summer, and Greg wonders how much he can stand his mother's planned fun, and dealing with the family's new dog, Sweetie. He would much rather be in front of the television or playing video games. As the summer progresses, Greg manages a little fun—things most middle-school kids would find boring. In *The Ugly Truth* (2010) Greg is in transition between childhood and full-blown adolescence, and he is searching for a new best friend after he and Rowley had a disagreement over the summer. To make matters worse, his family is making too many suggestions about his behavior and how he should be more responsible. *Cabin Fever* (2011), the sixth book in the series, is set between Thanksgiving and Christmas. When a snowstorm shuts off the electricity at the Heffley house, Greg is housebound with only his brothers for company. There's a lot of nonsense and sibling rivalry going on, and Greg once again records it all, words and pictures, in his faithful diary. *Third Wheel* (2012) has Greg reflecting on his life. To hear him tell it, he has suffered great trauma because he was forced to do things like babysit and participate in "take your kid to work day." Now his attempts to get a date for the school Valentine's Dance backfire, and he's right back in the middle of another embarrassing situation. Greg is still looking for a friend to replace Rowley in *Hard Luck* (2013). Rowley has captured the girls' eyes, and Greg can't manage a glimpse from them. He's spending more time with his family and some very weird relatives. When he can't manage to find a new pal, he tries to befriend Fregley, the class weirdo. That doesn't go so well, and Greg is once again down and out with "hard luck." He seems doomed to remain "wimpy."

*Diary of a Wimpy Kid: Greg Heffley's Journal* garnered rave reviews: *Booklist* (April 1, 2007) says, "At every moment, Greg seems real," and call it a "laugh-out-loud novel." *School Library Journal* (April 1, 2007) states that Greg is "oblivious to his faults that make him such an appealing hero." The starred review in *Publisher's Weekly* (March 5, 2007) says that Kinney's "print debut should keep readers in stitches, eagerly anticipating Greg's further adventures."

The *School Library Journal* (March 1, 2008) review of *Rodrick Rules* praises the humorous illustrations for capturing "characterizations and details not mentioned in the words." *Voice of Youth Advocates* (June 1, 2008) says, "The comedy is enhanced by lots of "exaggeration and stereotypical characters."

The third in the series, *The Last Straw,* draws praise from reviewers: *School Library Journal* (April 1, 2009) calls the voice "witty" and lauds the "memorable characterization." The reviewer for *Publishers Weekly* (January 19, 2009) finds Kinney's humor "spot-on" and praises the "winning formula of the deadpan text."

In the *Publishers Weekly* (October 12, 2009) review of *Dog Days* (2009), the reviewer says, " Kinney's gift for telling, pitch-perfect details in both his writing and his art remains." *Booklist* (October 15, 2009) states that there are "nods to reality" in Greg's summer vacation which "add humor and depth to this title."

*Booklist* (December 1, 2010) says of *The Ugly Truth,* "Kinney remains unerringly attuned to the tween psyche." *Publishers Weekly* (November 11, 2013) states, "Kinney once again gets in plenty of funny jabs at pop culture and everyday kid life."

The sixth book in the series is *Cabin Fever. Publishers Weekly* (November 14, 2011) says, "Kinney continues to excel at finding the innate humor in broadly relatable situations." The reviewer for *Kirkus* (December 1, 2011) says that Kinney "plays it safe" with this book, and therefore fails the reader. *Booklist* (December 1, 2011) states, "Kinney once again taps into kids' everyday emotions with uncanny accuracy and consistency."

*Booklist* (December 15, 2012) states that in *Third Wheel* Kinney "knows exactly how to make readers of all stripes ecstatic." *Horn Book Guide* (October 7, 2013) calls the book "authentic middle-school humor."

The *Publishers Weekly* (November 11, 2013) review of *Hard Luck* says that Kinney sticks to the same "situational humor" so popular in the earlier books. *Booklist* (December 1, 2013) says, "As ever, Kinney strikes his comic target in the bull's eye."

## CHALLENGES

In 2009 the series was challenged at the J. C. Martin Elementary School in the Laredo (Texas) Independent School District because it was deemed "politically, racially, or socially offensive." The status of the challenge is unknown.

The series was challenged, but retained at the Benignus Elementary School in the Klein (Texas) Independent School District in 2010. The person challenging the series was offended because it was "politically, racially or socially offensive." In the same year, *The Ugly Truth* was challenged in North Carolina because the book "promotes dishonesty, bullying, and lack of respect for parents; racism and culturally insensitive." The status of the challenge is unknown.

The series has also been challenged internationally in 2014. Australian Prime Minister Tony Abbott said that he wants the books out of schools. "What we don't want is weak, lame-ass pansies passing through our school system." He also claims the books are "not in touch with values of most Australian families."

## AWARDS AND ACCOLADES

### Diary of a Wimpy Kid: Greg Heffley's Journal

    2010  Garden State Children's Book Award: Children's Fiction
          (New Jersey)
    2010  Young Reader's Choice Award: Junior Books (Pacific
          Northwest)
    2010  West Virginia Children's Choice Award
    2009  Blue Spruce Award: Junior Book (Colorado)
    2009  Great Stone Face Children's Book Award (New Hampshire)
    2009  Indian Paintbrush Children's Book Award (Wyoming)
    2009  Kentucky Bluegrass Award: Grades 3–5
    2009  Maine Student Book Award
    2009  North Carolina Children's Book Award: Junior Books
    2008  Buckeye Children's Book Award: Grades 3–5 (Ohio)

### Diary of a Wimpy Kid: Rodrick Rules

    2011  Garden State Children's Book Award: Children's Fiction
          (New Jersey)

### Diary of a Wimpy Kid: The Last Straw

    2012  Blue Spruce Young Adult Book Award (Colorado)
    2010  Golden Archer Award: Intermediate (Wisconsin)

### Diary of a Wimpy Kid: Dog Days

    2012  Garden State Children's Book Award: Children's Fiction
          (New Jersey)
    2011  Golden Archer Award: Intermediate (Wisconsin)
    2009  Nevada Young Reader's Award

### Diary of a Wimpy Kid: The Ugly Truth

2013 Garden State Children's Book Award: Easy-to-Read (New Jersey)

2012 Golden Archer Award: Intermediate (Wisconsin)

### Diary of a Wimpy Kid: Cabin Fever

2014 Garden State Children's Book Award: Easy-to-Read (New Jersey)

2013 Golden Archer Award: Intermediate (Wisconsin)

### Diary of a Wimpy Kid: The Third Wheel

2012 ALA/YALSA Quick Picks for Reluctant Readers

## AUTHOR'S OFFICIAL WEBSITE

www.wimpykid.com

## FURTHER READING

### The Author

"Author Chat with Jeff Kinney." New York Public Library, August 19, 2008. www.nypl.org/author-chat-jeff-kinney.

"Jeff Kinney." *Contemporary Authors* online, 2011. Books and Authors. Gale.

"Jeff Kinney." FamousAuthors.org. www.famousauthors.org/jeff-kinney.

McCarron, Heather. "Nothing 'Wimpy' about Local Author's Success." *Milford Daily News* (Massachusetts), October 12, 2009. www.milford dailynews.com/x2118273676/Nothing-Wimpy-about-local-authors -success.

### The Book

Hunt, Jonathan. "Worth a Thousand Words." *Horn Book Magazine* 84 (July/August 2008): 421–26.

Renaud, Jeffrey. "Jeff Kinney Shares Secret Origin of 'Diary of a Wimpy Kid.'" *Comic Book Resources,* October 2013 (updated November 2013). www.comicbookresources.com/?page = article&id = 48709.

### Censorship

*All Things Considered.* "Some Parents Wary of 'Wimpy Kid' series," October 22, 2009. Transcript. www.npr.org/templates/story/ story.php?storyId = 114051484.

McCabe, Cynthia. "Is All Reading Good?" National Education Association. www.nea.org/home/37954.htm.

## For Listening and Viewing

www.scholastic.com/kpwebcast. *Scholastic.* This is an interview with Jeff Kinney and Dav Pilkey before they work live with students from New York City to create an original story.

www.readingrockets.org/books/interviews/kinney. *Reading Rockets.* This is a video interview with Jeff Kinney.

https://www.nbclearn.com/writersspeak/cuecard/60817. *Writers Speak with Kids,* September 17, 2012. Jeff Kinney speaks directly to kids about the *Diary of a Wimpy Kid* series.

## TALKING WITH READERS ABOUT THE ISSUES

- Define *wimp.* How does Greg Heffley fit the definition?
- How realistic is Greg's middle-school experience? Discuss how his experience is different from Rowley's. Explain why some adults find the books "socially offensive." Does this mean they are offended by middle-school behavior?
- Kids find the books very funny. What makes them so hilarious? How do the drawings add to the humor? Explain how middle-school humor is different from adult humor. Is that why many adults don't understand the popularity of the series?
- Some adults don't get the format of the books, and think that they aren't "good" literature. Support the argument that format doesn't dictate what is "good."
- Others have questioned the books because they feel that Greg's diaries promote "dishonesty, bullying, and lack of respect for parents." Debate whether an act of bullying in a book translates to bullying behavior in real life.
- How do you answer an adult who finds Greg gross and disrespectful?

## RELATED BOOKS CHALLENGED FOR SIMILAR REASONS

*Gantos, Jack.* **Joey Pigza Swallowed the Key.** *New York: Farrar, Straus and Giroux, an imprint of Macmillan, 1998.*

According to the Texas ACLU 2008–2009 Report of Banned and Challenged Books, this novel was challenged, but retained at the Clear Creek Intermediate School in the Sanger Independent School District because of "children behaving badly."

*Schrag, Ariel, ed.* **Stuck in the Middle: 17 Comics from an Unpleasant Age.** *New York: Penguin, an imprint of Penguin Random House, 2007.*

This collection of stories in comic format has been challenged in Dixfield, Maine, because of issues related to bullying, rejection, and depression—things many middle-school kids face. The school board voted in 2012 to restrict the book to readers with written parental permission. It was removed from the shelves of two Sioux Falls, South Dakota, middle schools in 2009 for the same reasons.

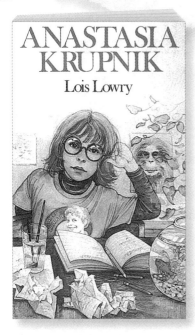

*Lois Lowry*
*Decorations by Diane de Groat*

## Anastasia Krupnik
*Boston: Houghton Mifflin, 1979*

## Anastasia Again!
*Boston: Houghton Mifflin, 1981*

## Anastasia at Your Service
*Boston: Houghton Mifflin, 1982*

*ANASTASIA KRUPNIK, ANASTASIA AGAIN!* AND *ANASTASIA AT YOUR SERVICE* are the first, second, and third of a nine-book series featuring Anastasia, a character that *Horn Book Magazine* called (December 1979) "one of the most intriguing female protagonists to appear in children's books since the advent of *Harriet the Spy.*" Reviewers consistently remark on Lowry's ability to fuse the comic and the serious in these books.

Anastasia is ten and on the brink of numerous changes when readers first meet her in *Anastasia Krupnik.* She loses her only-child status when her little brother, Sam, is born. And she is greatly affected by the declining mental state of her grandmother who no longer recognizes her. According to *Booklist* (October 15, 1979), "Humor filters through the dialogue as superbly developed characters react to the vicissitudes of life; and through them Lowry creates situations that can give a reader insight."

Anastasia is twelve years old and in the sixth grade in *Anastasia Again!* Her family has outgrown their city apartment and makes the decision to move to the suburbs. Once again, Anastasia's world is about to turn upside down. She has never lived in a house, and she will have to make new friends. Things start looking up for her when she meets the cute boy who lives down the street. *Kirkus* (October 1, 1982) says, "This is a sequel that gives us a maturing but no less spanking-keen heroine."

In *Anastasia at Your Service,* Anastasia hasn't lived in the suburbs long enough to make many new friends. At loose ends when summer begins, she decides to find work. She advertises herself as a "lady's companion," but the job she lands turns out to be more a maid than companion, and she discovers that her employer is the grandmother of a classmate. *Booklist* (September 1, 1982) says that Lowry is "right on target in capturing the thoughts and emotions of a twelve-year-old girl." *Horn Book Magazine* (December 1982) praises Lowry's "lively picture of a happy, devoted family."

Other books in this series: *Anastasia, Ask Your Analyst* (1984), *Anastasia on Her Own* (1985), *Anastasia Has the Answers* (1986), *Anastasia's Chosen Career* (1987), *Anastasia at This Address* (1991), and *Anastasia, Absolutely* (1995).

## CHALLENGES

The entire series was 29th on the American Library Association's 100 Most Challenged Books 1990–2000 for references to beer, *Playboy* magazine, and a casual reference to suicide.

The first documented challenge to *Anastasia Krupnik* was in 1986 at the Roosevelt Elementary School library in Tulare, California. The principal removed the book when a parent complained about the language (the phrase "crock of shit" appears twice in the book). The book was later returned to the shelves with the word "shit" covered with White-Out.

There was an unsuccessful challenge in 1991 in Wichita, Kansas, for being "offensive."

The book was removed at a Stevens Point (Wisconsin) elementary school in 1992 for "profanity and occasional references to underage drinking." The decision was reversed later in the year under condition that parents be given recommended reading lists containing descriptive paragraphs on the book's content.

In 1998 the novel was removed from the library shelves in one elementary school in Cayce-West Columbia, South Carolina, for "use of a vulgarity for human waste." This case prompted the school board to revise the school district's selection policy to include appropriateness of language in buying decisions.

The ALA's Office for Intellectual Freedom recorded a challenge in 2007 because the novel is "sexually explicit." The institution involved asked to remain anonymous.

*Anastasia Again!* was removed from an elementary school in Lake Wales, Florida, in 2005 because of a complaint that the book's references to "beer, *Playboy* magazine, and Anastasia making light of wanting to kill herself were inappropriate for children." There are additional anonymous challenges in 2007 that accuse the book of being "sexually explicit."

*Anastasia at Your Service* was challenged in 1984 in the Casper, Wyoming, school libraries by a couple who accused the book of being "subtle and filthy," and an instrument that "sexually and socially pervert, abuse, and scandalize innocent children."

## AWARDS AND ACCOLADES

2011    May Hill Arbuthnot Lecture
2001    Sutherland Lecture, Chicago Public Library
1979    Parents' Choice Awards: Fiction

## AUTHOR'S OFFICIAL WEBSITE

www.loislowry.com

## FURTHER READING

### The Author

Bonnheim, Julia N. "Lois Lowry Has the Answers: Remembering Reading Groups with Cambridge Author." *The Harvard Crimson,* April 17, 2003. www.thecrimson.com/article/2003/4/17/lois-lowry-has-the-answers-pretend/#.

Doll, Jen. "A Conversation with Lois Lowry." *The Atlantic Wire,* October 4, 2012. www.theatlanticwire.com/entertainment/2012/10/conversation-lois-lowry/57604.

"Lois Lowry." *Contemporary Authors* online, 2013. Books and Authors. Gale.

Silvey, Anita. "The Unpredictable Lois Lowry." *School Library Journal* 53, no. 6 (April 2007): 38–42.

## The Book

Kimmel, Eric A. "Anastasia Agonistes: The Tragicomedy of Lois Lowry." *Horn Book Magazine* 63 (March/April 1987): 181–87.

Vardell, Sylvia M. "The Role of Family in the Novels of Lois Lowry." *Children's Literature Remembered,* 187–200. Littleton, CO: Libraries Unlimited, 2003.

Zaidman, Laura M. "Journeys of Discovery in Lowry's Novels." *Bookbird* 35 (Summer 1997): 29–32.

## Censorship

"School Committee Votes to Ban Lowry Book." *The Ledger* (Lakeland, FL), February 24, 2005. www.theledger.com/article/20050224/NEWS/502240409.

## For Listening and Viewing

www.adlit.org/authors/Lowry. *AdLit,* January 24, 2011. Lois Lowry talks about her childhood.

www.readingrockets.org/books/interviews/lowry. *Reading Rockets.* Lois Lowry talks about her childhood and her love of words.

## TALKING WITH READERS ABOUT THE ISSUES

- In *Anastasia Krupnik,* Anastasia visits her dad's poetry class and hears a college student use an expletive. How does she react?
- Some libraries have chosen to mark out expletives in the Anastasia books. How is this worse than talking about words and how they define the characters that use them?
- How is Anastasia a typical adolescent? Why do you think people object to such adolescent behaviors?
- To what scenes are the censors referring when they say the books are "sexually explicit"?
- How would you defend the books to librarians, teachers, and principals who insist that the books are inappropriate for young adolescents?

## RELATED NOVELS CHALLENGED FOR SIMILAR REASONS

Blume, Judy. **Are You There God? It's Me, Margaret.** *New York: Random House, 1986 (first published by Bradbury, 1970).*

This book has numerous challenges because of the "honesty" about the adolescent experience. It was challenged in Bozeman, Montana, school libraries in 1985 because it is "profane, immoral, and offensive."

Fitzhugh, Louise. **Harriet the Spy.** *New York: Delacorte, a division of Random House, 2014 (first published by Harper and Row, 1964).*

In 1964 the novel was blackballed from the Association of Library Service to Children's Notable Children's Books list because of "mild profanity," and Harriet's independent nature. It was later included on a Notable Notables list. In 1983 it was challenged in the Xenia, Ohio, school libraries because the book "teaches children to lie, spy, back-talk, and curse."

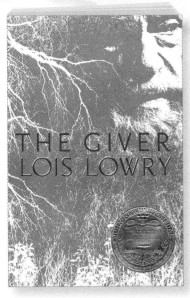

*Lois Lowry*

# The Giver

*Boston: Houghton Mifflin, 1993*

**SET IN THE FUTURE IN A DYSTOPIAN SOCI**ety where all individuals practice Sameness and where everything is colorless and void of emotions, the twelve-year-olds are about to receive their assignments, or occupations, from the Council of Elders. Assigned a number at birth, the children in the community are given a name in the Ceremony of the Ones. At twelve they are lined up by their original numbers and await their fate. Jonas, the main character, is apprehensive about the Ceremony of Twelves, and is puzzled when they skip over him and move methodically through the group making assignments until they reach the last number. Then Jonas's number is called and he is given his life assignment—Receiver of Memory. When Jonas begins his training with the former Receiver, who is now known as the Giver, he receives pleasant memories—sunsets, sailing, holidays—that existed before Sameness. Eventually he is forced to experience unpleasant emotions—sadness, loneliness, and pain. His isolation grows as he begins to experience things his family and friends will never experience.

Jonas is forced to make a decision that will affect his future when he learns that Gabriel, a baby his family has been tending, is to be "released" for failing to thrive. Before becoming the Receiver, Jonas thought that being "released" meant going to Elsewhere. Now he understands that it means death. To make matters worse, Jonas's father, who is a Nurturer, is assigned to do the release.

At the end of *The Giver* Jonas takes Gabriel and escapes to "Elsewhere." The reader is left to wonder whether Jonas and Gabriel survive the journey. If so, where are they? There are now three other books that answer that question for readers: *Gathering Blue* (2000), *Messenger* (2004), and *Son* (2012).

*Horn Book Magazine* (July 1993) says, "The story is skillfully written; the air of disquiet is delicately insinuated." *Voice of Youth Advocates* (August 1, 1993) calls it "a powerful story." They also say, "It should take its place with Orwell's *1984*." The reviewer for *School Library Journal* (May 1, 1993) recommends the book for grades 6–9 and says, "This tightly plotted story and its believable characters will stay with readers for a long time." *Publishers Weekly* (February 15, 1993) says that readers "will be easily seduced by the chimera of this ordered, pain-free society."

6 6 It always seems ironic to me that the book of mine most
challenged [*The Giver*] is the one about a drab, gray
world in which literature no longer exists. Books have
been removed, one by one, over years, for the most
horrifyingly benevolent of reasons: to make people feel
comfortable and safe."

—Lois Lowry, author of The Giver

## CHALLENGES

In the decade 1990–2000, *The Giver* was the American Library Association's 14th most challenged book.

The first recorded challenge to *The Giver* came in 1994 soon after the novel won the Newbery Medal. In that year, it was banned from classes by the Bonita Unified School District in La Verne and San Dimas, California, after four parents complained that "violent and sexual passages" were inappropriate for children.

In 1995 the novel was restricted to students with parental permission at the Columbia Falls (Montana) school system because of the themes of infanticide and euthanasia. In the same year, a parent in Franklin County, Kansas, challenged the book, citing "degradation of motherhood and adolescence." The book was removed from the school libraries, but available to teachers.

In 1996 it was challenged at the Lakota High School in Cincinnati, Ohio. The result of the challenge is unknown.

There were several public challenges in 1999. A pastor objected to the book's "mature themes"—suicide, sexuality, and euthanasia—at Troy

Intermediate School in Avon Lake, Ohio. It was also challenged, but retained, at a Lake Butler (Florida) middle school because "issues of infanticide and sexual awakening" are discussed in the book. Additional challenges recorded by Marshall University include Johnson County, Missouri, because it "desensitized children to euthanasia"; Sidney, New York, because of "mind control, selective breeding, and the eradication of the young when they are weak, feeble and of no more use"; and, in Oklahoma because of the terms "clairvoyance," "transcendent," and "guided imagery."

There continues to be challenges in the twenty-first century. In 2001 the Pickens, South Carolina, school board voted to ban the novel in elementary classrooms after a parent complained that euthanasia isn't an appropriate topic for children. The book remained in school libraries.

In 2003 the novel was challenged as suggested reading for eighth-grade students in Blue Springs, Missouri. Parents called the book "lewd" and "twisted" and pleaded for it to be tossed out of the district. The book was reviewed by two committees and recommended for retention, but the controversy continued in 2005.

The novel was challenged, but retained at the Seaman (Kansas) Unified School District 345 elementary school library in 2006. The result of the challenge is unknown.

Appalled by descriptions of "adolescent pill-popping, suicide, and lethal injections given to babies and the elderly," two parents demanded that the Mt. Diablo School District in Concord, California, eliminate the book from the school reading lists and libraries in 2007.

## AWARDS AND ACCOLADES

2013 May Hill Arbuthnot Lecture
2007 Margaret A. Edwards Award
2006 *Instructor Magazine* Named *The Giver* in Top 50 Kids Books Ever
1999 Virginia Readers' Choice Award: Middle School
1997 Buckeye Children's Book Award (Ohio)
1997 Land of Enchantment Book Award (New Mexico)
1996 Black-Eyed Susan Book Award (Maryland
1996 Great Stone Face Children's Book Award (New Hampshire)
1996 Rebecca Caudill Young Readers Award (Illinois)

1996   Sequoyah Book Award (Oklahoma)
1996   William Allan White Award (Kansas)
1995   Grand Canyon Reader Award (Arizona)
1995   Maine Student Book Award
1995   Pennsylvania Young Reader's Choice Award
1994   John Newbery Award
1994   ALA Notable Children's Books

## AUTHOR'S OFFICIAL WEBSITE

www.loislowry.com

## FURTHER READING

### The Author

Albert, Lisa Rondinelli. *Lois Lowry: The Giver of Stories and Memories.* Berkeley Heights, NJ: Enslow, 2007. 104 p. (Authors Teens Love Series)

Kois, Dan. "The Children's Author Who Actually Listens to Children." *New York Times Magazine,* October 3, 2012. www.nytimes.com/ 2012/10/07/magazine/lois-lowry-the-childrens-author-who-actually -listens-to-children.html?pagewanted = all.

"Lois Lowry." *Contemporary Authors* online, 2013. Books and Authors. Gale.

Lorraine, Walter. "Lois Lowry." *Horn Book Magazine* 70 (July/August 1994): 423–26.

Lowry, Lois. "The May Hill Arbuthnot Honor Lecture: Unleaving: the Staying Power of Gold." *Children and Libraries* 9, no. 2 (Summer 2011): 20–28.

Lowry, Lois. "The Zena Sutherland Lecture: The Remembered Gate and the Unopened Door." *Horn Book Magazine* 78, no. 2 (March/April 2002): 159–77.

Smith, Amanda. "PW Interviews: Lois Lowry (Writer of Young Adults' Books)." *Publishers Weekly* 229 (February 21, 1986): 152–53.

## The Book

Gann, Linda A., and Karen Gavigan. "The Other Side of Dark." *Voice of Youth Advocates* 35, no. 3 (August 2012): 234–38.

Lea, Susan G. "Seeing Beyond Sameness: Using 'The Giver' to Challenge Colorblind Ideology." *Children's Literature in Education* 37 (March 2006): 51–67.

Lowry, Lois. "Margaret A. Edwards Award Acceptance Speech: A Passionate Yearning." *Young Adult Library Services* 6, no. 1 (Fall 2007): 22–25.

Lowry, Lois. "1994 Newbery Acceptance Speech." *Journal of Youth Services in Libraries* 7 (Summer 1994): 361–67. Also appears in *Horn Book Magazine* 70 (July/August 1994): 414–22.

Silvey, Anita. "The Unpredictable Lois Lowry." *School Library Journal* 53, no. 6 (April 2007): 38–47.

Walters, Karla. "Other Voices: Pills against Sexual 'Stirrings' in Lowry's *The Giver*." *Bookbird* 32 (Summer 1994): 35–36.

## Censorship

Baldassarro. R. Wolf. http://bannedbooks.world.edu/2011/03/27/banned-books-awareness-giver-lois-lowry.

Bird, Betsy. "Top 100 Children's Novels #4: *The Giver* by Lois Lowry." *School Library Journal* (June 23, 2012). http://blogs.slj.com/afuse8production/2012/06/23/top-100-childrens-novels-4-the-giver-by-lois-lowry.

"The Giver." *Newsletter on Intellectual Freedom* 50 (September 2001): 192–93.

"Suicide Book Challenged in Schools." *USA Today,* July 20, 2001. http://usatoday30.usatoday.com/life/books/2001–07–20-the-giver.htm.

## For Listening and Viewing

www.youtube.com/watch?v=jvzsaK6z_WM. (Speech) June 2. 2012. Lois Lowry speaks at the Children's Book and Author Breakfast at Book Expo (2012).

www.loc.gov/podcasts/bookfest12/podcast_lowry.html. Published May 9, 2013. This is a podcast of Lois Lowry from the 2012 National Book Festival in Washington, DC.

**TALKING WITH READERS ABOUT THE ISSUES**

- Jonas doesn't know Sameness until he becomes the Receiver of Memory. How does being the Receiver add conflict to his life?
- How does Jonas's assignment change his relationship with friends and family?
- Why do you think The Giver shows Jonas the videotape of his father's release of the baby twin? Debate whether this scene foreshadows Jonas's decision in the end.
- The novel has been challenged for "desensitizing children to euthanasia." How does Jonas's decision to take Gabriel and leave the community make children more sensitive to issues of euthanasia?
- Other complaints of the novel are related to sexuality and adolescence. What are the "stirrings"? How is this normal in adolescent development?
- Why do adults get so nervous and hung-up about sexual feelings in adolescents? Debate whether Jonas's community is suppressing development by dispensing pills for the "stirrings."

**RELATED BOOKS CHALLENGED FOR SIMILAR REASONS**

*Collins, Suzanne.* **The Hunger Games trilogy.** *New York: Scholastic, 2008.*

The entire trilogy was #3 on the American Library Association's Top Ten Most Challenged Books List in 2012. Set in a dystopian society, the complaints include "anti-family," "sexually explicit," "violence," and "inappropriate for age group."

*Shusterman, Neal.* **Unwind.** *New York: Simon and Schuster, 2009.*

Removed from the curriculum, but retained in school libraries in Montgomery County, Kentucky, in 2010 for "inappropriate language and content."

*Phyllis Reynolds Naylor*

## Shiloh

*New York: Atheneum, a division of Simon and Schuster, 1991*

SET IN FRIENDLY, WEST VIRGINIA, AN abused beagle follows eleven-year-old Marty Preston along the winding Appalachian Mountain roads near the old Shiloh schoolhouse. Marty's father believes that the dog belongs to Judd Travers, a man noted for abusing his dogs. In Appalachia, people mind their own business and Marty's father insists that he return the dog to Judd. When Marty sees Judd, a drinking man, kick his dogs and shout profanities at them, he is faced with a moral dilemma. He can lie to his parents and hide Shiloh in a pen on the back part of their property, or he can allow Shiloh to be victim of Judd's abuse. He elects to keep the beagle and saves food from his own dinner to feed him. When another dog attacks Shiloh, Marty's secret is revealed. Marty and his dad take Shiloh to Doc Murphy to be mended, but Marty is once again told that he must return the dog to Judd Travers. This time Marty blackmails Judd into selling him Shiloh after he witnesses Judd shooting deer out of season. Though a deal is cut, Judd isn't a man of his word and Marty has to come up with other ideas for saving the dog.

*Publishers Weekly* (July 12, 1991) states, "Marty's tale is well told, with a strong emphasis on family and religious values." Ellen Mandel, reviewer for *Booklist* (December 1, 1991), says, "Naylor offers a moving and powerful look at the best and the worst of human nature as well as the shades of gray that color most of life's dilemmas." *Kirkus* (September 1, 1991) calls the novel "a gripping account of a mountain boy's love for a dog." The reviewer for *School Library Journal* (September 1, 1991) is lukewarm about the merits of the book, but does credit the book for a mixture of "honesty and personal relations." Leona Fisher praises Naylor in *Children's Literature Association Quarterly* (Spring 2003): "Marty's first-person narration in present tense is a remarkably unusual and compelling narrative strategy." She also acknowledges Naylor's "success in using dialect in the narration." Newbery Medalist Sharon Creech says that her favorite Newbery is *Shiloh.* In *Horn Book Magazine* (July/September 2012) she writes, "I admire its purity and poignancy and Naylor in rendering complexity with seeming simplicity." *Five Owls* (January/February 1992) reviewer Kathie Cerrra writes, "We know Marty's perceptions through vivid sensory detail, and we participate in his inner life of thought and feeling." She also makes a comment about the dialect, "The style of this book convincingly reflects regional speech and is spare and inviting."

*Shiloh Season* (1996) and *Saving Shiloh* (1997) bring Shiloh's story to a satisfying end. Warner Bros. produced a film of *Shiloh* (1996) that is available on DVD.

> " I'm constantly amazed that some people assume that children will do anything a character does in a book. I don't believe they will add "hell" to their vocabulary because Judd Travers says it in *Shiloh*, any more than Judd's mistreatment of his dogs means they will start kicking the family pet."
>
> —Phyllis Naylor, author of *Shiloh*

## CHALLENGES

A teacher at Oakdale Elementary School in Rock Hill, South Carolina, wrote to Phyllis Reynolds Naylor in 1993 and expressed concerns voiced by parents and students about the "profanity and the behaviors rewarded" in the novel.

In 1994 the book was challenged at Grayson Elementary School in the Caldwell (Louisiana) Parish School District. The objection was for profanity and the parent felt that students would be "embarrassed if read orally in front of the class." The superintendent also stated that the book took "God's name in vain several times." The greater issue in his eyes is the "ethical theme it portrayed." The book was removed from use with a fourth-grade class.

The 2003–2004 Annual Report of the Texas ACLU states that a Jewish parent brought a challenge to the book when his son was asked to read it. His objection was "a reference to praying to Jesus." The student was given an alternative assignment.

## AWARDS AND ACCOLADES

2000    *Shiloh* trilogy: National Education Association Top 100 Children's Book List

1999    Recommended Novel for Ages 9–12 in the Read Across America Initiative

1995    Buckeye Children's and Teen Book Award (Ohio)

1995    Delaware Diamonds: Intermediate (Gr. 3–5)

1994    Flicker Tale Children's Book Award (North Dakota)

1994    Grand Canyon Reader Award (Colorado)

1994    Indian Paintbrush Book Award (Wyoming)

1994    Land of Enchantment Book Award (New Mexico)

1994    Massachusetts Children's Book Award

1994    Nutmeg Children's Book Award (Connecticut)

1994    Sequoyah Children's Book Award (Oklahoma)

1994    Mark Twain Readers Award (Missouri)

1994    Nene Award (Hawaii)

1994    Rebecca Caudill Young Reader's Award (Illinois)

1994    Texas Bluebonnet Award

1994    West Virginia Children's Choice Book Award

1994    William Alan White Children's Book Award (Kansas)

1994    Young Hoosier Book Award: Intermediate Books (Indiana)

1994    Young Reader's Choice Award (Pacific Northwest)

1993    Dorothy Canfield Fisher Book Award (Vermont)

1993    Great Stone Face Children's Book Award (New Hampshire)

1993    Maine Student Book Award

1993    Pennsylvania Young Reader's Choice Award: Gr. 6–8

1992    John Newbery Medal

1991    American Library Association's Notable Children's Books

## OFFICIAL PUBLISHER WEBSITE

http://authors.simonandschuster.com/Phyllis-Reynolds-Naylor/
1792384

## FURTHER READING

### The Author

Graham, Joyce L. "An Interview with Phyllis Reynolds Naylor." *Journal of Youth Services in Libraries* 6 (Summer 1993): 392–93.

Naylor, Rex. "Phyllis Reynolds Naylor." *Horn Book Magazine* 68 (July/August 1992): 412–15.

"Phyllis Reynolds Naylor." *Contemporary Authors* online, 2013. Books and Authors. Gale.

### The Book

Fisher, Leona W. "I'm Thinking How Nothing Is as Simple as You Guess: Narration in Phyllis Reynolds Naylor's *Shiloh*." *Children's Literature Review* 135, no. 28.1 (Spring 2003): 17–25. Gale Literature Resource Center.

Mills, Claudia. "The Structure of the Moral Dilemma in *Shiloh*." *Children's Literature* 27 (1999): 185–97.

Naylor, Phyllis Reynolds. "1992 Newbery Acceptance Speech." *Journal of Youth Services in Libraries* 5 (Summer 1992): 351–56. Also appears in *Horn Book Magazine* 68 (July/August 1992): 404–11.

Naylor, Phyllis Reynolds. "The Writing of *Shiloh*." *Reading Teacher* 46, no. 1 (September 1992): 10–12.

### Censorship

Staino, Rocco. "Ellen Hopins, Phyllis Reynolds Naylor and Chirs Finan Are Honored for Their Roles Battling Literary Censorship." *School Library Journal* (November 19, 2012). www.slj.com/2012/11/events/ellen-hopkins-phyllis-reynolds-naylor-and-chris-finan-are-honored-for-their-roles-battling-literary-censorship/#.

West, Mark I. "Speaking of Censorship: An Interview with Phyllis Reynolds Naylor." *Journal of Youth Services in Libraries* 18 (Winter 1997): 177–82.

## For Listening and Viewing

www.readingrockets.org/books/interviews/naylor. *Reading Rockets.* This video interview with Phyllis Reynolds Naylor talks about the real Shiloh.

## TALKING WITH READERS ABOUT THE ISSUES

- Religion is important to the Preston family. How does Marty call upon his religious training when he is sorting out the lies that he tells?
- Describe Judd Travers. How does the description of his appearance, the way he abuses his dogs, and his use of profanity fit his character?
- What is Marty's ethical and moral dilemma?
- What does Mrs. Preston teach her children about giving someone a second chance? How does Marty give Judd Travers a second chance by the end of *Saving Shiloh*, the third book in the trilogy?
- The novel is written in Appalachian dialect, and has been the focus of some adult complaints. How are dialect and grammar different? Read aloud a paragraph in Standard English. How does changing the language affect the tone of the novel, and the sense of place?

## RELATED BOOKS CHALLENGED FOR SIMILAR REASONS

O'Hara, Mary. **My Friend Flicka.** New York: HarperCollins, 1948 (reissued 2008).
In 1990 the book was removed from a fifth- and sixth-grade reading list in Clay County, Florida, schools because of the words "bitch" in reference to a female dog, as well as the word "damn."

*Peck, Robert Newton.* **Soup.** *New York: Knopf, 1974.*

Challenged in 1992 as a fourth-grade reading assignment at the Woodbridge, New Jersey, schools for objectionable language and because "it teaches children how to lie, manipulate, steal, and cheat."

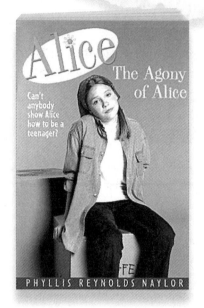

*Phyllis Reynolds Naylor*

## Alice series

*New York: Simon and Schuster, 1985–2013*

**ALICE MCKINLEY WAS ONLY FIVE YEARS OLD** when her mother died, leaving her in the loving care of her father and older brother, Lester. Aunt Sally, who lives in Chicago, is always available by telephone if Alice has "girl" types of questions, but Aunt Sally proves too conservative for the "honest" answers that Alice needs. In *The Agony of Alice,* the first book in the series, Alice is in sixth grade and has just moved to Silver Springs, Maryland, where her father is the manager of a music store. She is worried about making friends and adjusting to a new school. Alice makes it through sixth grade without too much trauma, and in the second book, *Alice in Rapture, Sort Of,* Alice and her new best friends, Pamela and Elizabeth, get their first boyfriends. In the books that follow, Alice grows chronologically and faces the many challenges that come with adolescence. There are typical spats with friends, breakups with boyfriends, and issues related to curfews and social functions. As a high school student, Alice becomes aware of social issues and begins to ponder what she can do to make a difference. When her school becomes embroiled in a censorship case, Alice becomes passionate about free speech rights. She recognizes racial bigotry and wants to fix it. She sees bullying and wants to face the bully.

There are sad times as well. A friend is killed in a car accident; another is dealing with cancer and chemotherapy treatments. One friend faces an unwanted pregnancy; another has a shotgun wedding. The final book, *Now I'll Tell You Everything,* brings Alice's life full circle. At the beginning of the novel she is entering her freshman year at the University of Maryland and by the last chapter Alice has turned sixty.

In the *Booklist* (March 15, 1985) starred review, *The Agony of Alice*, the first in the series, is called "a wonderfully funny and touching story." The *Boston Globe* states the novel has "breezy dialogue and a solid story line." *School Library Journal* (January 1, 1986) states, "Alice's forthcoming fans will agonize with her and await her future adventures."

*The Bulletin of the Center for Children's Books* (May 1994) praises *Alice In-Between* for "energetic dialogue and sprightly episodes." The starred review calls the novel "fresh."

*Publisher's Weekly* (May 1, 2000) says that Naylor, in *The Grooming of Alice,* "masterfully imparts physical, social, and emotional information while bringing readers to tears and laughter."

*Kirkus* reviews *Alice Alone* (May 1, 2001) and states that Alice "is blessed with a more loving family than many" and she continues to "get through the hard days as well as the good ones as best she can." Hazel Rochman, who has reviewed a number of the "Alice" books for *Booklist* (April 1, 2007) says of *Dangerously Alice,* "Teens will love the funny, honest, non-messagey drama on the edge." *School Library Journal* (August 1, 2007) calls the book "episodic" though "fans will surely snatch it up."

*School Library Journal* (June 1, 2010) states, "Alice is a wonderful role model" in *Alice in Charge.* Rochman writes for *Booklist* (May 15, 2010) "Avoiding formulas, Naylor breaks new ground again."

*Kirkus's* review of *Incredibly Alice* (May 10, 2011) states, "As ever, Naylor-as-Alice fills the interstices with teachable moments."

The reviewer for *School Library Journal* (July 1, 2012) says of *Alice on Board* "avid *Alice* fans will want this next-to-last installment." *Voice of Youth Advocates* (June 1, 2012) calls the book "an enjoyable beach read for teens."

Ann Kelly reviews *Now I'll Tell You Everything* in *Booklist* (August 2013) and states, "Naylor has given fans a gift: the chance to see how life unfolds for a beloved character."

## The *Alice* Books

*The Agony of Alice,* 1985
*Alice in Rapture, Sort Of,* 1989
*Reluctantly Alice,* 1991
*All but Alice,* 1992
*Alice in April,* 1993
*Alice In-Between,* 1994

*Alice the Brave,* 1995

*Alice in Lace,* 1996

*Outrageously Alice,* 1997

*Achingly Alice,* 1998

*Alice on the Outside,* 1999

*The Grooming of Alice,* 2000

*Starting with Alice,* 2002

*Alice in Blunderland,* 2004

*Lovingly Alice,* 2006

*Simply Alice,* 2002

*I Like Him, He Likes Her,* 2010—This multivolume edition contains
       *Alice Alone* (2001), *Simply Alice,* and *Patiently Alice* (2003)

*Alice on Her Way,* 2005

*It's Not Like I Planned It This Way,* 2010—This multivolume edition
       contains *Including Alice* (2004), *Alice on Her Way* (2005),
       and *Alice in the Know* (2006)

*Dangerously Alice,* 2007

*Almost Alice,* 2008

*Intensely Alice,* 2009

*Alice in Charge,* 2010

*Incredibly Alice,* 2011

*Alice on Board,* 2012

*Now I'll Tell You Everything,* 2013

## CHALLENGES

In 2003, the *Alice* series topped the American Library Association's Most Challenged Books List because of "sexual content, offensive language and unsuited to age group." The series was the second most challenged in 2002 because of "homosexuality, sexually explicit scenes and unsuited to age group." In 2006 the series was named the third most challenged for "offensive language and sexually explicit scenes;" and in 2011 the series made #6 on the Most Challenged List for "nudity, offensive language, and religious viewpoint." The American Library Association, the American Civil Liberties Union, and the National Coalition Against Censorship record the following specific challenges:

*Achingly Alice, Alice in Lace,* and *The Grooming of Alice* were banned from the Webb City (Missouri) school library in 2002 because the book "promotes homosexuality and discusses issues 'best left to parents.'" It was also banned at the middle school in the Lumberton (Texas) Independent School District because it is "sexually explicit."

*The Agony of Alice* was challenged in 2000 at the Franklin Sherman Elementary School library and on the Fairfax, Virginia, County approved reading list. The book was retained in libraries but limited in its classroom use to small group discussion and for girls only.

*Alice Alone* and *Patiently Alice* were moved in 2006 from the Junior High School Library to the Senior High School Library in the Katy (Texas) Independent School District.

*Alice on Her Way* was challenged at the Icicle River Middle School Library in Leavenworth, Washington, in 2008. The book was retained, but restricted to students who have parental consent to read it. In 2010 the Texas ACLU reported that the novel was placed on a restricted shelf at Sealy Junior High School in the Sealy Independent School District because of "sexual content and nudity."

*Alice on the Outside* was challenged in 2005, but retained in the librarian's office at the Shelbyville East Middle School in Kentucky because the book is "too sexually explicit" for middle-school students. The book is available with parental permission. According to the Texas ACLU, this book was banned in 2011 at Goliad Elementary School in the Eastland Independent School District.

*Alice the Brave* was challenged in the Mesquite Pirrung Elementary School library in Texas in 2004 due to "sexual references."

*Alice In-Between* was removed from the Monroe, Connecticut, sixth-grade required reading list after some parents called attention to the book's "sexual content."

*All but Alice* was restricted to students with parental permission at the Monroe Elementary School library in Thorndike, Maine, in 1997. The novel was removed in the same year from the elementary school libraries in the Rosemount-Apple Valley-Eagen Independent School District #196 in Minnesota because of a "brief passage in which the seventh-grade heroine discusses sexually oriented rock lyrics with her father and older brother."

*Dangerously Alice* was banned in elementary schools, placed on restricted shelves in middle schools, and retained in high schools in 2010 in the Beaumont (Texas) Independent School District. According to the Texas ACLU, the school district had issues with the "sexual content or nudity" in the book and felt it "offensive to religious sensitivities."

*Intensively Alice* was challenged at Buffalo Prairie Middle School in Buffalo, Missouri, in 2013 because a grandmother, a teacher, and the principal felt the book was "pornographic and/or obscene." The book was retained after the American Library Association and the Missouri Library Association became involved.

*Lovingly Alice* was challenged in 2005 because the book contains highly "inappropriate graphic sex content" at Quail Run Elementary School in the Paradise Valley (Arizona) Unified School District, and in 2011 the book was removed. The novel was banned for "sexual content" in 2006 at the Bens Branch Elementary School in the New Caney (Texas) Independent School District.

*Alice on Her Way* was restricted to students with parental permission at the Icicle River Middle School in Leavenworth, Washington, in 2008. The reason given was that the book is "objectionable."

*Alice on the Outside* was challenged in Shelbyville, Kentucky, in 2005 because the book is "too sexually explicit for middle school students." The superintendent "determined that the book would be available only in the librarian's office and students could request it with parental permission." It was banned in 2010 at Goliad Elementary School in the Eastland Independent School District, Texas, because of "profanity, sexual content or nudity."

*Reluctantly Alice* was challenged in 2006 in Wake County Schools, North Carolina, by parents who sought support from Called2Action, a Christian group that says its mission is to "promote and defend our shared family and social values."

## AWARDS AND ACCOLADES

2012  Naylor is Honored by the National Coalition Against Censorship for fighting censorship

2011  *Alice in April:* IRA/CBC Children's Choices

1998  *Outrageously Alice:* ALA Best Books for Young Adults; VOYA Best Books for Young Adults

1994  *Alice in April:* ALA Reluctant Young Adult Readers

1993  *All but Alice:* ALA Notable Books for Children; IRA/CBC Children's Choices;

1992  *All but Alice:* School Library Journal Best Books of the Year

1991  *Reluctantly Alice:* School Library Journal Best Book

1986  *Agony of Alice:* ALA Notable Children's Books

## AUTHOR'S OFFICIAL WEBSITE

http://alicemckinley.wordpress.com

## FURTHER READING

### The Author

Fetterhoff, Whitney. "Interview with Children's Author Phyllis Reynolds Naylor." *Washington Post,* June 6, 2011. www.washingtonpost.com/ lifestyle/style/interview-with-childrens-author-phyllis-reynolds -naylor/2011/06/02/AGDT0YKH_story.html.

"Phyllis Reynolds Naylor." *Contemporary Authors* online, 2013. Books and Authors. Gale. www.scholastic.com/teachers/contributor/phyllis -reynolds-naylor. Scholastic.

### The Books

Devereaux, Elizabeth. "An Appetite for *Alice.*" *Publishers Weekly* 249, no. 39 (September 30, 2002): 26–27.

Flynn, Kitty. "Everygirl: Phyllis Reynolds Naylor's Alice." *Horn Book Magazine* 83, no. 5 (September/October 2007): 463–67.

Hesse, Monica. "Closing the Book on 'Alice.'" *The Washington Post,* October 14, 2013.

Jones, Carolyn E. "For Adults Only? Searching for Subjectivity in Phyllis Reynolds Naylor's *Alice* Series." *Children's Literature Association Quarterly* (Spring 2005): 16–31.

Naylor, Phyllis Reynolds. "To Be Continued . . . . . ." *Horn Book Magazine* 82, no. 1 (January/February 2006): 41–44.

Scales, Pat. "Because of Alice: Phyllis Reynolds Naylor's *Alice* Books." *Book Links,* a supplement of *Booklist* (June 2011): 14–17.

### Censorship

Bronson, Andrea. "Teens' Favorite Authors Face Book Bans." *We News,* October 22, 2007. http://womensenews.org/story/books/071022/ teens-favorite-authors-face-book-bans#.UxthI9xOF4M.

Gounley, Thomas. "At Principal's Request, Buffalo Middle School to Consider Banning Novel." *News-Leader* (Springfield, MO), March 2, 2013. www.news-leader.com/article/20130302/NEWS01/ 303020053/Buffalo-Middle-School-book-ban.

Staino, Rocco. "Ellen Hopkins, Phyllis Reynolds Naylor, and Chris Finan Are Honored for Their Roles in Battling Literary Censorship." *School Library Journal,* November 19, 2012. www.slj.com/2012/11/events/ellen-hopkins-phyllis-reynolds-naylor-and-chris-finan-are-honored -for-their-roles-battling-literary-censorship.

West, Mark. "Speaking of Censorship: An Interview with Phyllis Reynolds Naylor." *Journal of Youth Services* in Libraries (Winter 1997): 177–82.

### For Listening and Viewing

www.readingrockets.org/books/interviews/naylor. *Reading Rockets.* In this video, Naylor reflects on her childhood and love of stories.

## TALKING WITH READERS ABOUT THE ISSUES

- At what point does Alice realize that Aunt Sally is too conservative to answer some of her questions? How does she feel more comfortable asking questions of her cousin, Carol? Why does every girl need someone to talk with about "girl" topics?
- The Alice books have been challenged in school and public libraries because of "sexual content." How are the books a good source of information for girls?
- Many schools include sex education in the curriculum. Explain the rationale of a school board that votes to teach sex education, but insists that fiction that deals with adolescents' curiosity about sex be removed from the shelves of the library.
- Alice comes face to face with social issues that most adolescents witness in their schools: bullying, book censorship, homosexuality, drugs and alcohol use, unwanted pregnancies. Why do these issues make some adults nervous? How does Alice deal with these issues? Explain how "not knowing" is more dangerous than "knowing" about these topics.

## RELATED NOVELS CHALLENGED FOR SIMILAR REASONS

*Brashares, Ann.* **Sisterhood of the Traveling Pants.** *Delacorte, an imprint of Penguin Random House, 2001.*

In 2010, the ALA's Office for Intellectual Freedom recorded a challenge to the novel because it's "sexually explicit and unsuitable to age group," and in 2007 and 2005 there were challenges that charged "offensive language." An additional challenge was filed in 2004 because the book is "sexually explicit," "contains offensive language," "promotes drugs, alcohol, and smoking," and is considered " unsuitable to age group."

*Mackler, Carolyn.* **Love and Other Four Letter Words.** *Delacorte, an imprint of Penguin Random House, 2009.*

In 2001 this novel was removed from the Lincoln Junior High School in Naperville, Illinois, because in addition to swear words and discussions about "getting wasted," the book contains "graphic passages about masturbation and sexual intercourse."

*Barbara Park*

# Junie B. Jones series

*Illustrated by Denise Brunkus.*
*New York: Random House, 1992–2013*

**JUNIPER BEATRICE JONES IS HER REAL** name, but she wants to be called Junie B. When Junie B. is in kindergarten, her two best friends are Lucille, a very pretty rich girl, and Grace, an African American girl who is a good athlete. Junie B. is sometimes bossy and often poorly behaved. She tries the patience of her teacher, whom she calls "Mrs.," and the principal, who is simply "Principal." Even her parents get worn out with her antics, like being convinced that there is a monster under her bed, or when she plays beauty shop and cuts her hair. While she is in kindergarten, her mother gives Junie B. a baby brother, but being a big sister doesn't seem to improve her behavior. She is notorious for her "mispronunciations" of words that most kindergarteners know, and she has terrible grammar. On the eve of kindergarten graduation, Junie B. starts to think about being a first grader, and she frets about her new glasses and the lunch for her new lunchbox. Once school starts and Junie B. is settled into Mr. Scary's first-grade classroom, she suffers a great disappointment. Her desk is next to May Murkee, who is a big fat tattletale. She has also traded allegiances. She dumps Lucille and Grace, or they dump her, and her new best friends are Herb, Jose, and Lennie.

Junie B. and her classmates take a field trip to the farm, produce a play for Columbus Day (Junie B. plays a ship), and they celebrate all of the usual holidays. Through it all, Junie B. still gets into "giant messes" and continues to use baby talk and poor grammar. She is her teachers' nightmare, while also giving them plenty of laughs.

*Publisher's Weekly* (July 20, 1992) recommends *Junie B. Jones and the Stupid Smelly Bus* for ages 6–9 and states, "Park convinces beginning readers that Junie B.—and reading—are lots of fun." *School Library Journal* (November 1, 1992) says, "It's a real hoot." In the *Booklist* (November 15, 1993) review of *Junie B. Jones and Her Big Fat Mouth,* the reviewer says that Junie B. "veers from catastrophe to rapture." Ilene Cooper, reviewer for *Booklist* (March 1, 1993), says that *Junie B. Jones and A Little Monkey Business* is a "cross between Ramona and Eloise."

*Junie B. Jones Has a Monster under Her Bed* doesn't impress the reviewer for *School Library Journal* (November 1, 1997) who states that Junie B.'s "personality is more annoying than endearing." *School Library Journal* (January 1, 2002) says of *Junie B., First Grader (at Last!),* "As always, Park is in touch with what the kids know and how they feel." *The Horn Book Guide* (April 1, 2003) reviews *Junie B., First Grader: Toothless Wonder,* and says "Brunkus's comical drawings suit the text."

The reviewer for *School Library Journal* (September 1, 2003) says of *Junie B., First Grader—Cheater Pants,* "The story wraps up nicely." *Booklist* (September 15, 2003) states, "Park creates a wonderful classroom of distinct personalities." The reviewer for *Booklist* (July 1, 2002) says that Junie B. is "still sassy, hilarious, and insightful" in *Junie B. Jones: Boss of Lunch.* *School Library Journal* (March 2004) says that *Junie B., First Grader: One Man Band* is "treated with humor and hope."

## THE *JUNIE B. JONES* SERIES

### Kindergarten

*Junie B. Jones and the Stupid Smelly Bus,* 1992
*Her Big Fat Mouth,* 1993
*A Little Monkey Business,* 1993
*Some Sneaky Peeky Spying,* 1994
*The Yucky Blucky Fruitcake, 1995*
*That Meany Jim's Birthday,* 1996
*Jones Loves Handsome Warren,* 1996
*Is Not a Crook,* 1997
*Has a Monster under Her Bed,* 1997
*Is a Party Animal,* 1997
*Is a Beauty Shop Guy,* 1998
*Smells Fishy,* 1998

*Is (Almost) a Flower Girl,* 1999
*The Mushy Gushy Valentine,* 1999
*Has a Peep in Her Pocket,* 2000
*Is Captain of Field Day,* 2000
*Is a Graduation Girl,* 2001

**First Grade**

*Junie B., First Grader (at Last!),* 2001
*Boss of Lunch,* 2003
*Toothless Wonder,* 2003
*Cheater Pants,* 2003
*One Man Band,* 2003
*Shipwrecked,* 2004
*Boo . . . and I MEAN IT!* 2004
*Jingle Bells, Batman Smells (P.S. So Does May),* 2005
*Aloha-ha-ha!,* 2006
*Dumb Bunny,* 2007
*Turkeys We Have Loved and Eaten (And Other Thankful Stuff),* 2012
*B. My Valentine,* 2013
*Essential Survival Guide to School,* 2013

❝ I happen to think that a book is of extraordinary value if it gives the reader nothing more than a smile or two. In fact, I happen to think that's huge."

—Barbara Park, author of the *Junie B. Jones* series
(from http://juniebjones.com/author)

**CHALLENGES**

According to the ALA's Office for Intellectual Freedom, not one specific title, but the entire series was #71 on the 2000–2009 Top 100 Banned or Challenged Books because of "poor social values," "not a good role model," and "bad spelling and grammar." In 2004 Barbara Park was named one of the Top Ten Most Challenged Authors.

A parent challenged *Junie B. Jones and the Stupid Smelly Bus* in 1998 at the Harmony Township, New Jersey, school. The challenge states that the book "sends a message to children that extreme emotions such as hate are fine, and the book never resolves any of the issues it raises or points out that there are ways to handle negative emotions constructively." The book was retained.

According to the 2003–2004 Texas ACLU Annual Report of Banned and Challenged Materials, the entire series was challenged, but retained at the Webb Middle School in Austin, Texas, because Junie B. speaks "nonstandard English."

In 2006 *Junie B. Jones and Some Sneaky, Peaky Spying* was challenged in the Wake County School District, North Carolina, for the reasons that have caused the entire series to be challenged in other libraries and school districts. The result of the challenge is unknown.

## AWARDS AND ACCOLADES

*Junie B., First Grader (at Last!)*
2002  ABC Children's Booksellers Choices Awards

*Junie B. Jones Is Not a Crook*
2001  Delaware Diamonds Primary Award (Grades K–2)

*Junie B. Jones and the Stupid Smelly Bus*
1998  Golden Archer Award: Primary (Wisconsin)
1995  Great Stone Face Children's Book Award (New Hampshire)

*Junie B. Jones and Her Big Fat Mouth*
1996  Nevada Young Reader's Award

## PUBLISHER'S OFFICIAL WEBSITE

http://juniebjones.com
www.randomhousekids.com/brand/junie-b-jones

## FURTHER READING

### The Author

"Barbara Park." *Instructor* 117 (January/February 2008): 72.
"Barbara Park." *Contemporary Authors* online, 2014. Books and Authors. Gale.
www.rif.org/kids/readingplanet/bookzone/park.htm. Reading Is Fundamental.

https://www.scholastic.com/teachers/contributor/barbara-park. Scholastic.

## The Books

Blais, Jacqueline. "Junie B. Always Has the Bestest Time." *USA Today,* June 30, 2004. http://usatoday30.usatoday.com/life/books/ news/2004–06–30-junieb_x.htm.

Wickstrom, Carol D., Joan Scott Curtis, and Kayla Daniel. "Ashley and Junie B. Jones: A Struggling Reader Makes a Connection to Literacy." *Language Arts* 83, no. 1 (September 2005): 16–21.

## Censorship

Grossman, Anna Jane. "Is Junie B. Jones Talking Trash?" *New York Times,* July 26, 2007. www.nytimes.com/2007/07/26/fashion/26junie .html?pagewanted = all&_r = 0.

Jones, Stephanie. "Language with an Attitude: White Girls Performing Class." *Language Arts* 84, no. 2 (November 2006): 114–24.

Ratzan, Jill S. "You Are Not the Boss of My Words! Junie B. Jones, Language and Linguistics." *Children and Libraries* 3, no. 3 (Winter 2005): 31–38.

Trelease, Jim. "Challenging Captain Underpants and the Irrepressible Junie B. Jones. Updated March 30, 2011. www.trelease-on-reading .com/censor7.html#underpants.

## TALKING WITH READERS ABOUT THE ISSUES

- Why is Junie B. Jones so funny?
- Some adults don't like that Junie B. mispronounces words, or that she uses bad grammar. How does her grammar improve by the time she reaches first grade?
- Describe Junie B.'s behavior. How does she act in ways that you aren't allowed? Is that what makes her funny? What would she be like as a friend? What would you like to tell Junie B. about her behavior?
- How is Junie B. like a lot of kindergarteners and first-graders? Describe times when her teachers and the principal are impatient with her. How does Junie B. also amuse them?

- Junie B. sometimes uses the word "stupid." Think about a different word for Junie B. to use. Does changing the word change the story?

## RELATED BOOKS CHALLENGED FOR SIMILAR REASONS

*Allard, Harry.* **The Stupids Die.** *Illustrated by James Marshall. Boston: Houghton Mifflin, 1974.*

Complaints that "children shouldn't call anyone 'stupid'" resulted in the removal of this book and other titles in the series in 1998 at the Howard Miller Library in Zeeland, Michigan.

*Callen, Larry.* **Just-Right Family: Cabbage Patch Kids series.** *Pawtucket, RI: Parker Brothers, a division of Hasbro, 1984.*

"Ungrammatical writing" was the reason this book was challenged in 1987 at the Rutherford County Elementary School in North Carolina.

*Todd Parr*

# The Family Book

*New York: Megan Tingley Books, an imprint of Little, Brown and Company, 2003*

IN BRIGHT, BOLD, AND CHILDLIKE ILLUSTRATIONS OF PEOPLE AND ANIMAL characters, this simple concept book for preschool children, and those just learning to read, is all about family. There are big families and small ones. Some families have one mom or one dad. Others may have two moms or two dads. There are families that are tidy and others that are very messy. There are ones that are loud and ones that are quiet. Some families are only one color and others are different colors. Though families may be unalike, there are ways that they are the same. Most all families like sharing hugs, birthday celebrations, being together, and helping one another when they feel sad. The premise of the book is to get children engaged in a conversation about their own family, while understanding and appreciating that their friends may come from different types of families. The last page reveals the message that Parr wants to deliver: "There are lots of different ways to be a family. Your family is special no matter what kind it is."

*The Horn Book Guide* (April 1, 2004) calls the book "an ode to diversity." *Publisher's Weekly* (November 17, 2003) says the book makes "simple statements of tolerance and love." The reviewer for *School Library Journal* (December 1, 2003) calls the book "a concept book" that celebrates "the diversity of family groups."

## CHALLENGES

According to the Texas ACLU Annual Report of Challenged and Banned Books 2008–2009, there was a challenge at Caraway Elementary School

> **❝** I just want to inspire kids to feel good about who they are and learn about differences. I didn't invent the things I write about. I just try to make them easier to understand."
>
> —Todd Parr, author of *The Family Book*

in the Round Rock Independent School District that stated the book was "politically, racially, or socially offensive." It was retained.

There was a challenge reported in Texas in 2011, but the institution asked to remain anonymous.

In 2012 the book was removed from the elementary school library shelves in Erie, Illinois, because of one sentence: "Some families have two moms and two dads." According to the ALA's Office for Intellectual Freedom, there was an anonymous challenge in 2008, and in Pennsylvania in 2012.

### AWARDS AND ACCOLADES

2014　Reach Out and Read Mills-Tannenbaum Award for Children's Literacy

### AUTHOR'S OFFICIAL WEBSITE

www.toddparr.com

### FURTHER READING

#### The Author

"Family Guy." Advocate. www.advocate.com/politics/commentary/2006/04/10/family-guy.

Pearlman, Jeff. "Todd Parr." www.jeffpearlman.com/the-quaz-qa-todd-parr-2. Posted November 13, 2013.

"Todd Parr." *Contemporary Authors* online, 2013. Books and Authors. Gale.

"Todd Parr." *Instructor* 116 (March/April 2007): 72.

## The Book

http://uuathome.com/tag/the-family-book. Posted February 3, 2011.

## Censorship

Dahlstrom, Katie. "Book Still Banned in Erie." *Clinton Herald* (Clinton, Iowa), June 15, 2012. www.clintonherald.com/lifestyles/x1387 78703/Book-still-banned-at-Erie.

Mary Tyler Mom Blog. www.chicagonow.com/mary-tyler-mom/2012/ 06/erie-illinois-not-up-to-parr.

## For Listening and Viewing

http://wqad.com/2012/06/05/controversial-decision-in-erie-gathering -national-attention. This newscast video and accompanying article reports on the removal of *The Family Book* in Erie, Illinois.

http://ncacblog.wordpress.com/2012/06/04/the-story-behind-todd-parrs -the-family-book. Todd Parr talks about the story behind *The Family Book* on the National Coalition Against Censorship's blog.

www.youtube.com/user/toddparr. Todd Parr speaks to children.

www.youtube.com/watch?v = aW1Cn_EEnt8&list = UUrVYw0RG-Lip6D 7jhWdE_zQ. Reach Out and Read of Greater New York, March 24, 2014. Todd Parr talks about the importance of reading.

## TALKING WITH READERS ABOUT THE ISSUES

- Let's look at the book's cover. Describe the children in the picture. How are they alike? How are they different? Why do you think they are in a tree?
- Look around the classroom, or your story time group. How does everyone look different? But there are things that you all enjoy. Maybe it's a special book, or a game, or food. Let's talk about how we are alike.
- Describe different types of families in the book. The families in the book enjoy hugs. What else do the families enjoy? How do you know that the families love one another? How do they help one another?
- How is your family different from a friend's family? Let's talk about how "all families are special, no matter what kind it is."

## RELATED BOOKS CHALLENGED FOR SIMILAR REASONS

*Brown, Marc Tolon.* **Buster's Sugartime.** *New York: Little Brown Books for Young Readers, 2006.*

In 2009 the book was challenged, but retained at the Union, Oklahoma, district elementary school libraries despite a parent's complaint that the book features two same-sex couples and their children.

*Bruel, Nick.* **The Bad Kitty Christmas.** *New York: Roaring Brook Press, an imprint of Macmillan, 2011.*

The Texas ACLU Annual Report 2012–2013 states that the book was challenged at the Dickinson Elementary School in the Lamar Consolidated Independent School District because the "lesbian partners are holding a child and that it's unsuitable for elementary school." The book was retained.

Katherine Paterson

## *Bridge to Terabithia*

*New York: HarperCollins, 1977*

**JESS AARONS IS GOOD AT ART, AND NOT SO** good at things that most guys in his class enjoy. To make matters worse, his father disapproves of his art. Jess thinks that he can change things if he practices running during the summer and enters the big race on the first day of school. But he is surprised and humiliated when he loses the race to a newcomer and his new neighbor, Leslie Burke. Jess realizes that he will never be a good runner, but something worth more than a championship happens that changes his life. He and Leslie become friends, and together they create a secret hiding place they call Terabithia.

When Leslie drowns in a swollen creek while Jess is away on a museum trip to Washington, he is paralyzed with sadness. A bit of the magic of Terabithia is lost the day Leslie died, and Jess thinks about how he was nothing before Leslie came. He makes one final trip to Terabithia alone. This time, he makes a wreath of wildflowers and places it on the ground in Leslie's memory. Then he builds a bridge to Terabithia and leads May Belle, his little sister, across the bridge to the magical kingdom that Leslie helped create.

Jack Forman, reviewing for *School Library Journal* (November 1977), says, "Jess and Leslie are so effectively developed as characters that young readers might well feel that they were their classmates." The reviewer for *The Bulletin of the Center for Children's Books* (December 1977) writes, "Quite unlike Paterson's previous books in setting or theme, this is just as beautifully crafted and convincing, but even more touching." *Booklist* (November 15, 1977) calls the character portrayals and changing relationships superb.

## CHALLENGES

This Newbery Medal winner was #8 on the American Library Association's 100 Most Challenged Books list: 1990–2000. And in 2003 it was #10 on the Top Ten Most Challenged List for "offensive language," and because it "promotes the occult and Satanism."

The first recorded challenge to the novel was in Lincoln, Nebraska, in 1986. The book was questioned because it contains "profanity," including the phrase "Oh, Lord" and "Lord" used as expletives. In the same year, it was challenged as "unsuitable" for the curriculum in the Harwinton and Burlington, Connecticut, schools because it contains "language and subject matter that set bad examples and gives students negative views of life."

In 1992 it was challenged at the Mechanicsburg (Pennsylvania) Area School District because of profanity and reference to witchcraft.

A 1993 challenge in Oskaloosa, Kansas, led to a new policy mandating that teachers examine their required reading material for profanities. The new policy requires teachers to list each profanity and the number of times it is used in the book and forward the list to parents, who will be asked to give written permission for their children to read the material.

In 1995 a group of parents asked the Medway, Maine, school board to stop fifth-grade students from reading two books in class. The parents charged that *The Castle in the Attic* by Elizabeth Winthrop and *Bridge to Terabithia* "use swear words and deal with sorcery."

It was removed from the fifth-grade classrooms of the New Brighton Area School District in the Pulaski, Pennsylvania, Township in 1996 due to "profanity, disrespect of adults, and an elaborate fantasy world." Those bringing the challenge felt this might lead to confusion.

In 2002 the novel was challenged in the middle school curriculum in Cromwell, Connecticut, due to concern that it promotes "witchcraft and violence."

## AWARDS AND ACCOLADES

2013  Laura Ingalls Wilder Award
2000  *School Library Journal* One Hundred Books That Shaped the Century
1997  May Hill Arbuthnot Honor Lecture
1986  Blue Spruce Young Adult Book Award (Colorado)

1986   Le Grand Prix des Jeunes Lecturs (France)
1981   Janusz Korczak Medal (Poland)
1981   Silver Pencil Award (Netherlands
1978   John Newbery Medal
1978   Lewis Carroll Shelf Award
1977   American Library Association Notable Children's Book
1977   School Library Journal's Best Books of the Year


## AUTHOR'S OFFICIAL WEBSITE

http://terabithia.com


## FURTHER READING

### The Author

Brodie, Carolyn S. "Katherine Paterson: Noted Novelist for Young People."
    *School Library Monthly* 17 (May 2001): 45–47.
Brown, Jeffrey. "Conversation: Katherine Paterson, National Ambassador
    for Young People's Literature." *PBS NewsHour,* January 15, 2010.
    www.pbs.org/newshour/art/blog/2010/01/conversation-katherine
    -paterson-national-ambassador-for-young-peoples-literature.html.
Horning, Kathleen T. "Katherine the Great." *School Library Journal* 56
    (February 1, 2010): 26–29.
"Katherine Paterson." *Contemporary Authors* online, 2013. Books and
    Authors. Gale.
Paterson, Katherine. "May Hill Arbuthnot Honor Lecture: In Search of
    Wonder." *Journal of Youth Services in Libraries* 10 (Summer 1997):
    378–91.
Sutton, Roger. "An Interview with Katherine Paterson." *Horn Book
    Magazine* 86 (March 2010): 10–14.
Trierweller, Hannah. "Meet the Author: Katherine Paterson." *Instructor*
    116 (January/February 2007): 41–43.

### The Book

Bagnell, Norma. "Terabithia: Bridge to a Better World." *Language Arts* 56
    (April, 1979): 429–31.

Chattaway, Peter T. "Deeper into Terabithia." *Christianity Today* 51 (March 1, 2007): 64–67.

Hass, Elizabeth, and Patricia Light. "Reading about Death." *Parents* 60 (November 1991): 26–29.

Kingman, Lee. "Newbery and Caldecott Medal Books, 1976–1983 with acceptance papers, biographies, and related material chiefly from *Horn Book Magazine*." Boston: *Horn Book Magazine*, 1986.

Paterson, Katherine. "Hope and Happy Feelings." *Catholic Library World* 80 (July/August 1988): 14–18.

### Censorship

Deming, Nicole. "Katherine Paterson: The Risks of Great Literature." *Guernica,* October 2, 2012. www.guernicamag.com/daily/katherine -paterson-the-risks-of-great-literature.

Grogan, David. "Connecticut Residents Seek to Ban Two Newbery Medal Winners from School." *Bookselling This Week,* July 29, 2002. www .bookweb.org/news/connecticut-residents-seek-ban-two-newbery -medal-winners-school.

Hirsch, Karen. "*Bridge to Terabithia:* Too Good to Miss." In *Censored Books II: Critical Viewpoints, 1985–2000,* ed. Nicholas J. Karolides, 100–106. Lanham, Md: Scarecrow, a division of Rowman and Littlefield Publishing Group, 2002.

### For Listening and Viewing

www.youtube.com/watch?v = fMx0nsnr_oA. MovieSharing02. May 28, 2012. This is the full movie of *Bridge to Terabithia.*

www.readingrockets.org/books/interviews/paterson. *Reading Rockets,* 2011. This is a video interview with Katherine Paterson.

## TALKING WITH READERS ABOUT THE ISSUES

- There are objections to the novel because of "profanity." How is the language in the book authentic to the setting and characters? What is a writer's responsibility to create characters that are real to the world in which they live?
- Some adults have challenged the book because they feel that the imaginary kingdom of Terabithia is promoting "witchcraft." What is

the difference between an imagination and "witchcraft"? How is a
vivid imagination part of normal childhood play?

- There are also complaints that the book is "depressing." How does
Jesse deal with Leslie's death?
- To what are the censors referring when they accuse the book of
showing "disrespect of adults"?
- How does Leslie's death change Jess's relationship with his father?

## RELATED BOOKS CHALLENGED FOR SIMILAR REASONS

Bauer, Marion Dane. **On My Honor.** *New York: Clarion, 1986.*

In 1995 this book was challenged in fourth- to-sixth grade reading classes
in Grove City, Pennsylvania, because it was "depressing." It was challenged
in 1992 at the Alamo Heights School District in Texas because the book
uses the words "hell," "damn," and "frigging."

Park, Barbara. **Mick Harte Was Here.** *New York: Knopf, 1995.*

The book was challenged, but retained at the Centennial Elementary School
library in Fargo, North Dakota, after parents complained to school officials
that the book contains themes and language inappropriate for elementary
students. The book was also challenged, but retained at the Liberty Middle
School Library in Seneca, South Carolina, in 1998 after a seventh grader's
grandmother complained to school officials.

*Susan Patron*

# The Higher Power of Lucky

*New York: Richard Jackson Books/ Atheneum an imprint of Simon and Schuster, 2006*

FOR TEN-YEAR-OLD LUCKY TRIMBLE THE ONLY THING WRONG WITH HER LIFE IN Hard Pan, California, (population 43) is she doesn't have an actual mother. Instead she has Brigitte, her father's ex-wife and her legal guardian. The little trailer that Lucky and Brigitte call home is comfortable, but not very private. When Lucy overhears Brigitte's telephone conversations with her mother back in France, she becomes concerned that Brigitte is homesick. Her suspicions grow when she sees Brigitte's passport and legal documents spread out in full view. At this point, Lucky feels that the only way to avoid being placed with a foster family is to run away. She packs a survival kit and takes off. Things don't go exactly as planned because Lincoln and Miles, the only other kids in Hard Pan, the entire town, and one almost actual mother lead her home.

Lucky is brave, caring, smart, and full of curiosity. She enjoys hanging out with five-year-old Miles, who lives with his grandmother while his mother completes a prison term, and Lincoln, a knot-tying champion. The center of Hard Pan is the Found Object Wind Chime Museum. One day Lucky is cleaning up around the museum and overhears Short Sammy through the fence say that his dog got "bitten on the scrotum" by a rattlesnake. Lucky doesn't know what the word *scrotum* means, but at the end of the novel she finally asks. The museum also hosts the Twelve-Step anonymous meetings—alcoholics, gamblers, smokers, and overeaters. Lucky overhears Short Sammy talk about his "rock-bottom" moment with alcohol and how he finds his "higher power," but she doesn't understand how one actually finds it. A series of events unfold, and Lucky realizes that maybe everyone, including herself, can find their "higher power."

When Patron's novel was published in 2006, it won accolades from all the major reviewing journals. The starred review in *Kirkus* (October 15, 2006) calls the novel "a small gem." The *Booklist* (December 1, 2006) review says, "Patron's plotting is as tight as her characters are endearing. Lucky is a true heroine, especially because she's not perfect." Finally, the reviewer in *School Library Journal* (December 1, 2006) says the book is "one of hope and love."

Barbara A. Genco, formerly with the Brooklyn Public Library and currently with *School Library Journal,* confesses that at first she didn't give this novel much thought. After the 2007 Newbery Medal announcement, she took another look at the book. She writes on the "Goodreads" blog, "This is a terrific book and a cut (no pun intended) above the usual Newbery fare." She gives the book five stars.

Lucky's journey has grown into a trilogy. She is eleven years old in *Lucky Breaks* (2009) and more than anything she wants a girlfriend. She strikes up a friendship with Paloma Wellborne, a girl who comes to Hard Pan with her uncle to do geological research. Finally, in *Lucky for Good* (2011), Lucky must deal with questions that aren't easily answered: Does the father who abandoned her truly hate her? Is she really going to hell for studying Charles Darwin?

" It is misguided for librarians to want to protect young readers from words or concepts in books. If literature functions as a window to the human heart and as a door to the world, the goal of librarians should be to fling those doors and windows open: to connect kids with books, to respect their intelligence, and to stimulate and encourage reading. Children have reacted to Lucky's story in many positive ways; since its publication in 2006, no young reader has expressed any response at all to the word *scrotum* except to look it up in the dictionary."

—Susan Patron, author of *The Higher Power of Lucky*

**CHALLENGES**

Just weeks after *The Higher Power of Lucky* was named the Newbery winner, the *New York Times* reported that "the book has already been banned from school libraries in a handful of states in the South, the West and the Northeast, and librarians in other schools have indicated in the online debate that they may well follow suit" (www.nytimes.com/2007/02/18/books/18newb.html). The controversy started when a school librarian from Colorado posted on LM-Net, an online discussion group for school librarians worldwide, that she was concerned about the word *scrotum* in the novel. This prompted a discussion among subscribers about whether the book is appropriate for the targeted 9–12 age group. The reporter hijacked several other online discussion groups like Librarian.net and read various blogs. It's unclear if this is where she got the following response from a librarian at Halsted Middle School in Newton, NJ: "I think it's a good case of an author not realizing her audience. If I were a third- or fourth-grade teacher, I wouldn't want to have to explain that."

*The New York Times* article sent local, state, and regional newspapers scrambling to report their own version of the issue. There were radio talk shows that devoted entire programs to a discussion of the book. Many supported the book and accused the *Times* reporter of sensationalizing the issue. All of this was good fodder for a number of blogs, most of which can be easily accessed by doing a Google search of *The Higher Power of Lucky*—Censorship.

**AWARDS AND ACCOLADES**

    2007  John Newbery Medal
    2007  Notable Children's Books—Association of Library Service to Children, a division of the American Library Association
    2006  *Kirkus* Editor's Choice
    *New York Times* Best Seller List
    *Publisher's Weekly* Best Seller List
    *Booksense* (now called *IndieBound*) Best Seller List
    Barnes and Noble Best Seller List
    Amazon.com Best Seller List

## AUTHOR'S OFFICIAL WEBSITE

www.susanpatron.com

## FURTHER READING

### The Author

Oleck, Joan. "The Higher Power of Patron: Profile of Newbery Winner." *School Library Journal* 53, no. 5 (March 2007): 42–45.

"Susan Patron." *Contemporary Authors* online. Books and Authors. Gale. http://cynthialeitichsmith.blogspot.com/2007/12/author-interview -susan-patron-on-higher.html.

Walter, Virginia A. "Susan Patron." *Horn Book Magazine* 83 (July/August 2007): 337–39.

### The Book

Patron, Susan. "The Newbery Medal Acceptance Speech: The Bathtub Storyteller." *Children and Libraries* 5 (Summer/Fall 2007): 6–9. Also appears in *Horn Book Magazine* 83 (July/August 2007): 337–39.

http://latimesblogs.latimes.com/jacketcopy/2009/12/flashback-review -the-first-take-on-susan-patrons-newbery-winner.html.

www.latimes.com/news/opinion/commentary/la-oe-patron11–2009 jan11,0,2957320.story.

### Censorship

Bosman, Julie. "With One Word, Children's Book Sets Off Uproar." *New York Times,* February 18, 2007. www.nytimes.com/2007/02/18/ books/18newb.html?_r=0.

Patron, Susan. "Shock Treatment." *Horn Book Magazine* 83 (September/ October 2009): 581–87.

Schliesman, Megan. "Self-Censorship: Let's Talk About It." *Wisconsin Library Association Intellectual Freedom Roundtable Newsletter* (Spring 2007). https://ccbc.education.wisc.edu/freedom/selfcensorship.asp.

### For Listening and Viewing

www.youtube.com/watch?v=c_L9UEJ3X8g. February 5, 2010. This "90-Second Newbery: The Higher Power of Lucky, If Brigitte Had

Foreseen the Controversy" on YouTube is a conversation between Lucky and Brigitte about the word *scrotum*.

## TALKING WITH READERS ABOUT THE ISSUES

- What are your thoughts regarding the criticism of *The Higher Power of Lucky* because of the word *scrotum*? Explain why someone would be offended by the word, or laugh at it.
- Why do you think Patron chose to use the proper name of the body part rather than a slang term? Discuss why it is always better to use the correct word when referring to the anatomy.
- At the end of the novel, Lucky asks Brigitte to explain the word *scrotum*. What is symbolic about her question?
- Lucky learns about the Twelve-Step program for various addictions when she overhears Short Sammy and the other guys talking about their "rock bottom" moments. What is Lucky's rock bottom moment?
- How does Lucky's life change after she finds her Higher Power?
- Lucky wants to be a scientist and reads everything she can find on Charles Darwin. Explain why Darwin and his theories are controversial. Debate how reading about Darwin's theory of evolution could strengthen or weaken personal beliefs about science and religion.

## RELATED BOOKS CHALLENGED FOR SIMILAR REASONS

Colman, Hila. **Diary of a Frantic Kid Sister.** *New York: Crown Publishing, an imprint of Penguin Random House, 1973.*

In 1982, this novel was removed from the Hurst-Euless-Bedford School District libraries in Texas because the book uses the word *intercourse.*

Naylor, Phyllis Reynolds. **Alice, In Between.** *New York: Simon and Schuster, 1994.*

In 1998 this book was removed from the Monroe, Connecticut sixth-grade required reading list after some parents called attention to the book's sexual content. There is discussion between Alice and her friends about the male anatomy.

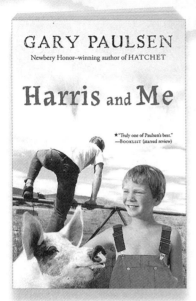

*Gary Paulsen*

## Harris and Me: A Summer Remembered

*Boston: Houghton Mifflin Harcourt Publishing Co., 1993*

AT DIFFERENT POINTS IN HIS LIFE, AN eleven-year-old boy is shipped off to stay with relatives because his alcoholic and abusive parents are too unfit to care for him. This summer a sheriff's deputy delivers him, along with a cardboard box filled with his belongings, to the Larsons' farm in a remote area of Minnesota. The boy is accustomed to city kids, so when he meets nine-year-old Harris, the Larsons' son, he isn't sure what to think. Harris is quick to blurt out anything that comes to mind, even when his older sister, Glennis, reminds him that certain questions aren't polite. Harris has a reputation for being rude and asks, "We heard your folks was puke drunks, is that right." The boy simply answers, "They drink too much." As the boy learns to follow along with Harris's schemes, he soon forgets the life he left behind. In the city he would never think to attach a washing machine motor to a bicycle. He would never have a wrestling match with a 300-pound pig, or be kicked in the butt by a cow.

Told in first person, the episodic chapters reveal the prankster Harris through the naive eyes of the unnamed city boy. Day after day, the boy is the victim of Harris's jokes, but late in the summer he figures out how to get revenge. He manipulates Harris into peeing on an electrical wire. The boy finds the scene hilarious, but Harris doesn't see it that way until much later. By now the boys are on equal terms, and by the end of the summer they are both sad when the sheriff's deputy returns to take the boy back to the city. On the drive home, the boy thinks about the pigs, the horses, the chores, swimming, and going to a Gene Autry movie. Most of all, he remembers his friend, the crude and cussing Harris who knows how to turn a summer into a barrel of laughs.

*School Library Journal* (January 1, 1994) says the stories are "memorable and humorous and very telling of human nature." The reviewer for *Voice of Youth Advocates* (February 1, 1994) says there is "instant rapport" between the two boy protagonists. *Publishers Weekly* (October 18, 1993) states, "Paulsen choreographs an antic jig of down-on-the-farm frolics in this warm comedy." *Kirkus* (October 15, 1993) calls the book "an earthy, wonderfully comic piece." Stephanie Zvirin, reviewer for *Booklist* (December 1, 1993), says that Paulsen proves himself "a top-notch humorist—as adept at capturing character eccentricities as he is at building momentum toward riotous climax." *The Bulletin of the Center for Children's Books* (January 1994) says the book is "one of the most optimistic fictional worlds to invite young visitors in a long while."

## CHALLENGES

The novel ranked #70 on the American Library Association's top 100 Most Challenged Books list 2000–2009. From 1996 to 2011, the American Library Association registered eight challenges to *Harris and Me.*

In 1997 it was challenged for "explicit language" in the Lander County School District in Nevada. The novel was retained. The book was challenged and removed in 2000 at District Central Heights Independent School District in Nacagdoches, Texas, as "sexually explicit."

In 2004 it was challenged at the Paulding County Carnegie Library in Ohio citing "offensive language and religious viewpoint." The outcome of this challenge is unknown.

In 2008 adults finding "objectionable content" in the novel succeeded in getting it restricted to students with parental permission at the Icicle River Middle School in Leavenworth, Washington.

In 2009 it was challenged at the Celina (Texas) Intermediate School for "cultural insensitivity, racism, nudity, offensive language, political viewpoint and sexually explicit." The outcome of this particular challenge is unknown.

The Oregon Intellectual Freedom Clearinghouse reported a challenge in a public library because of "sexually offensive language." The patron was also concerned that the book might encourage "alcoholism, use of offensive language, cruelty to animals and viewing pornography." There was a challenge registered with the American Library Association in 2011 for reasons similar to the complaints in previous years. The institution asked to remain anonymous.

## AWARDS AND ACCOLADES

2007   NEA Teachers' Top 100 Books for Children
1997   Margaret A. Edwards Award
1997   Golden Archer Award: Middle/Junior High School (Wisconsin)
1997   Iowa Teen Award
1997   South Carolina Young Adult Book Award
1996   Young Hoosier Award Middle Grades (Indiana)
1994   ALA-YALSA Best Books for Young Adults
1993   *Booklist* Editor's Choice

## OFFICIAL PUBLISHER'S WEBSITE

www.randomhouse.com/features/garypaulsen

## FURTHER READING

### The Author

Devereaux, Elizabeth." PW Interviews Gary Paulsen." *Publishers Weekly* 241 (March 28, 1994): 70–71.

"Gary Paulsen." *Contemporary Authors* online, 2013. Books and Authors. Gale.

Handy, Alice Evans. "An Interview with Gary Paulsen." *Book Report* 10 (May/June 1991): 28–31.

Macken, Joann Early. *Gary Paulsen: Voice of Adventure and Survival.* Berkeley Heights, NJ: Enslow, 2007. 104 p. (Authors Teens Love Series)

Salvner, Gary M. *Presenting Gary Paulsen.* New York: Macmillan, 1996. 176 p. (Twayne's United States Author Series).

Zvirin, Stephanie. "The *Booklist* Interview: Gary Paulsen." *Booklist* 95, no. 9–10 (January 1–15, 1999): 864–65.

## The Book

Bartky, Cheryl. "Write What You Are." *Writer's Digest* 74 (July 1994): 42–44, 65.

Wood, Susan Nelson. "Bringing Us the Way to Know: The Novels of Gary Paulsen." *English Journal* 90 (January 2001): 67–72.

## Censorship

Pritchard, T. Gail. "Banned Books: Some Explanations." http://wowlit.org/blog/2012/10/29/banned-books-some-explanations. October 29, 2012.

Salvner, Gary M. "A War of Words: Lessons from a Censorship Case." *Alan Review* 25 (Winter 1998). http://scholar.lib.vt.edu/ejournals/ALAN/winter98/salvner.htm.

## For Listening and Viewing

www.youtube.com/watch?v=Q7ADtOjxmRs. Random House Kids, June 6, 2010. Gary Paulsen discusses his life as a writer.

www.youtube.com/watch?v=BBhv-domQOA. December 13, 2010. Filmed by Ed Spicer, Gary Paulsen talks about his life and his books.

## TALKING WITH READERS ABOUT THE ISSUES

- *Harris and Me* often appears in bibliographies of humorous books. Discuss why it's so funny. Is it what the characters say, or what they do?
- The novel has been censored because of "offensive language." How does the language define Harris? At first, the boy doesn't quite know how to take Harris. At what point do the boys become best buddies?
- Explain why a challenger would say that the novel is "sexually explicit." How are these scenes typical adolescent behavior? What might you say to someone who makes this claim?
- Discuss why the book is challenged for "cultural insensitivity." The novel is set not too long after World War II. How does the era contribute to Harris's insensitivity?
- Explain why it's important for a person to understand that "profanity" and "cultural insensitivity" describes the book and the characters, not the reader.

## RELATED BOOKS CHALLENGED FOR SIMILAR REASONS

*Hiaasen, Carl.* **Hoot.** *New York: Knopf Books for Young Readers, an imprint of Penguin Random House, 2002.*

The Texas ACLU Annual Reports 2011–2012 states that this 2003 Newbery Honor Book was challenged at Coder Elementary School in the Aledo Independent School District because of "profanity, including damn and smartass." The book was retained.

*Paulsen, Gary.* **The Cookcamp.** *New York: Penguin Random House, 1990.*

In 2010 the novel was challenged, but retained at the Sinton Elementary School in the Sinton (Texas) Independent School District because of "sexual content or nudity."

*Peck, Robert Newton.* **Soup.** *New York: Knopf, an imprint of Penguin Random House, 1974. Available: info@learninglinks.com.*

In 1992, this book was challenged as a fourth-grade reading assignment at the Woodbridge, New Jersey, school because of "objectionable language" and "it teaches children how to lie, manipulate, steal, and cheat."

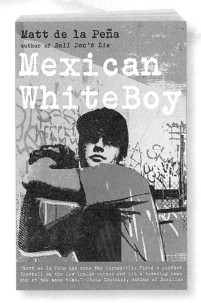

*Matt de la Peña*

# Mexican WhiteBoy

*New York: Delacorte, a division*
*of Penguin Random House, 2008*

**SIXTEEN-YEAR-OLD DANNY LOPEZ IS BUILT** like a baseball player. His long arms give him power on the pitcher's mound, and his 95-mile-an-hour fastball could earn him scholarship offers to colleges he never dreamed of attending. The problem is that Danny isn't on the baseball team at the elite all-white private school he attends. He didn't make the cut for the team because on the day of the tryouts his nerves got the best of him, and he threw balls far out of the strike zone. Because Danny is half-Mexican, the kids at school ignore him, and Danny feels that he doesn't really fit in. Danny's father hasn't been in his life for four years, but Danny wants to connect with his Mexican heritage and decides to spend the summer with his father's relatives in a poor, predominately Mexican neighborhood in San Diego while his mother is off with her rich boyfriend. Things aren't always good there because Danny doesn't speak Spanish, and he feels that his whiteness interferes with forming a good relationship with his relatives and the neighborhood kids.

When Danny meets Uno, a half-black/half-white boy whose father is also absent, the two form a friendship that sets them on a journey of self-discovery. Together they learn to face the demons that are holding them back on the baseball field and in life.

Lynn Rutan, reviewer for *Booklist* (August 1, 2008), says, "Danny's struggle to find his place will speak strongly to all teens but especially to those of mixed race." Madeline Walton-Hadlock states in *School Library Journal* (September 1, 2008) that "as the characters develop, their language starts to feel familiar and warm." Matthew Weaver, the reviewer for *Voice of Youth Advocates* (October 1, 2008), focuses on the many obstacles that the characters faces, and states "in a fantastic move by the author that is not cloying or obvious, they also have the temerity to overcome them." Safia Uddin, reviewer for *SIGNAL Journal* (Spring/Summer 2009) calls the novel "another engaging and perceptive read with realistic characters and authentic language."

" I always wanted to get banned. But when the Arizona thing happened, and I realized it was my target audience that wouldn't be able to read my books, I was devastated. The symbolism was inescapable: a book populated by Mexican-American characters was literally taken out of the hands of Mexican-American students and put in boxes in the basement."

—Matt de la Peña, author of Mexican WhiteBoy

### CHALLENGES

In 2012 the Tucson Unified School District (Arizona) shut down the successful Mexican-American Studies program, and books and materials were boxed and marked 'banned.'" *Mexican WhiteBoy* was one of the books. The school district labeled it "anti-American" and objected to a "fight scene." District authorities said that while the book had no place in the classroom, it was available in the school libraries.

### AWARDS AND ACCOLADES

2009 American Library Association Best Book for Young Adults (Top 10 Pick)
2009 Notable Books for a Global Society
2009 Texas Tayshas Reading List
2008 Bulletin of the Center for Children's Books Ribbon List
2008 Junior Library Guild Selection

## AUTHOR'S OFFICIAL WEBSITE

www.mattdelapena.com

## FURTHER READING

### The Author

Manfredi, Angi. "Talking about Your World." *Voice of Youth Advocates* 36 (August 2013): 14–17.

"Matt de la Peña." *Contemporary Authors* online, 2013. Books and Authors. Gale.

Murtagh, Heather. "Students Connect with Authors." *San Mateo Daily Journal* (California), November, 9, 2009. http://archives.smdaily journal.com/article_preview.php?id = 119439.

Peña, Matt de la. "Sometimes the 'Tough Teen' Is Quietly Writing Stories." NPR, November 11, 2013. www.npr.org/blogs/code switch/2013/11/11/243960103/a-reluctant-reader-turns-ya-author -for-tough-teens.

### The Book

Buehler, Jennifer. "Their Lives Are Beautiful, Too: How Matt de la Peña Illuminates the Lives of Urban Teens." *ALAN Review* 37 (Winter 2010). http://scholar.lib.vt.edu/ejournals/ALAN/v37n2/buehler .html.

Rudnicki, Alicia. "Longing to Belong: In *Mexican WhiteBoy* a Confused Teen Searches for Home Base." Examiner.com, December 23, 2009. www.examiner.com/article/longing-to-belong-mexican-whiteboy-a -confused-teen-searches-for-home-base.

### Censorship

Winerip, Michael. "Racial Lens Used to Cull Curriculum in Arizona." *New York Times,* March 19, 2012. www.nytimes.com/2012/03/19/ education/racial-lens-used-to-cull-curriculum-in-arizona.html?ref = education&_r = 0.

## For Listening and Viewing

www.teachingbooks.net/book_reading.cgi?id = 3842&a = 1. Matt de la
Peña talks about writing *Mexican WhiteBoy* and reads an excerpt
from the novel.

www.readwritethink.org/parent-afterschool-resources/podcast-episodes/
conversation-with-matt-pena-30322.html. This podcast is a conversation between Matt de la Peña and Professor Jennifer Buehler.

www.youtube.com/watch?v = 2WkDD_IpaEs.

www.youtube.com/watch?v = w_AgZ13Sj0Q&feature = relmfu.

www.youtube.com/watch?v = r-4d8s-1yg0&feature = relmfu.

www.youtube.com/watch?v = F-0X71Md7JM&feature = relmfu.
This four-part presentation by Matt de la Peña is sponsored by the
Center for Fiction in New York.

www.youtube.com/watch?v = NWURx3aZjSY. New York City Educators,
2012. This video features Matt de la Peña at an author event in New
York City.

## TALKING WITH READERS ABOUT THE ISSUES

- Define bigotry. What is the difference between overt and covert
  racism? Which type of racism does Danny face?
- Describe Danny's identity crisis. How is this related to a "label"
  placed on him by society?
- What is symbolic about the scene where Danny and Uno go to the
  train bridge and await an oncoming train? Debate whether this
  begins his journey or completes it.
- The state of Arizona shut down the Mexican American studies program in Tucson and banned *Mexican WhiteBoy*. Why do you think
  the politicians and school officials in Arizona were threatened by
  the novel?
- Some of the students spoke up and protested the politicians' action.
  How would you respond if this type of censorship occurred in your
  school or school system?
- What are proactive steps that teenagers can take to combat bigotry
  and racism in their school?

## RELATED BOOKS CHALLENGED FOR SIMILAR REASONS

Crutcher, Chris. **Whale Talk**. *New York: Greenwillow, a division of Harper-Collins, 2001.*

In 2007 this book was challenged at the Missouri Valley High School in Iowa because of "racial slurs and profanity." The superintendent of education in South Carolina removed it from the suggested reading list for a pilot English-literature curriculum in 2005.

Lipsyte, Robert. **The Contender.** *New York: HarperCollins, 1967.*

The novel was challenged in 2009 at Roach Middle School in the Frisco (Texas) Independent School District because it was deemed "politically, racially or socially offensive." The book was also challenged in New Jersey (2008) and Colorado (2003). The institutions involved ask to remain anonymous.

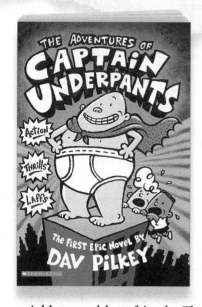

*Dav Pilkey*

## Captain Underpants series

*New York: Scholastic, 1997–present*

**GEORGE BEARD AND HAROLD HUTCHINS,** the fourth-grade class clowns in the Captain Underpants series, are next-door neighbors and best friends. They attend the Jerome Horwitz Elementary School where they have regular encounters with Mr. Krupp, the principal who hates kids. The school doesn't encourage fun or creativity and discourages any use of imagination. George and Harold remedy the situation by creating "Treehouse Comix, Inc.," their own comic book series that features a superhero called "Captain Underpants," an alter ego of Mr. Krupp. The captain is clad in white jockey shorts, sports a red cape, and flies around the school on various escapades. George and Harold love trouble, and in the first book, *The Adventures of Captain Underpants*, they put bubble bath in band instruments and fill footballs with helium. In the subsequent books, the pranksters manage to wreak havoc throughout the school from ruining the science fair to turning the cafeteria red by running over ketchup packets with their skateboards. The two even consider an idea to make a robot urinal, called "The Urinator." They manage to drive their science teacher into retirement and draw laughs about the new teacher's name, Professor Pippy P. Poopypants. The series is filled with villains like Mr. Meaner, the gym teacher, Miss Edith Anthrope, the school secretary, and Miss Singerbrain, the librarian who bans books.

In its review of *The Adventures of Captain Underpants*, *Publishers Weekly* (June 9, 1997) states, "Pilkey uses a sitcom-like formula to set up the rivalry between the boys and the principal and to strip the authority figure of dignity." The reviewer for *School Library Journal* (June 1, 1999) says of *Captain Underpants and the Attack of Talking Toilets*, "The fun is in the reading, which is full of puns, rhymes, and nonsense." *Booklist* (February 15, 2000) calls *Captain Underpants and the Preposterous Plight of the Purple Potty People* "silly, gross-out fun." *Publishers Weekly* (January 28, 2002) recommends *The Adventures of Super Diaper Baby* for ages 7–10, and states, "Pilkey's latest is replete with misspellings, pleasingly bad puns." The reviewer also calls attention to the very funny "flip-o-rama feature." *School Library Journal* (January 2012) recommends *Captain Underpants and the Invasion of the Potty Snatchers* for grades 2–4. The reviewer notes, "Crude humor is easy. Funny crude humor is not. And the laughs here (and there are many) are definitely spot on." In his *Booklist* (September 1, 2012) review of *Captain Underpants and the Terrifying Return of Tippy Tinkletrousers,* Andrew Medlar says that the book "combines empowerment and empathy with age-appropriate humor and action." *School Library Journal* (October 1, 2012) calls it a silly book, but thinks the "anti-bullying messages" are worthwhile.

## CHALLENGES

The book series was #1 on the American Library Association's Top Ten Most Frequently Challenged Books List in 2013, #8 in 2005, #4 in 2004, and #6 in 2002. The reasons given include "offensive language, unsuited for age group, violence."

In 2000 the entire series was removed from the Maple Hill School in Naugatuck, Connecticut, because of "unruly behavior among children." It was also challenged, but retained at the Orfordville (Wisconsin) Elementary School Library. A parent charged that the books teach "students to be disrespectful; not to obey authority, including God's law; improper spelling; to make excuses and lie to escape responsibility; to make fun of what people wear; and poor nutrition."

*Captain Underpants and the Perilous Plot of Professor Poopy Pants* was removed from the Page School in the Hope-Page (North Dakota) Consolidated School District in 2002. A former teacher brought the challenge and stated, "I didn't care for the language. I didn't care for the innuendos."

In 2003 the book was challenged, but retained in the Riverside (California) Unified School District classrooms and libraries, despite a complaint about the book's "inappropriate" scatological storyline.

*Captain Underpants and the Super Diaper Baby* was removed from Harvey S. Brown Elementary School in Channelview, Texas, in 2011 after parents complained that their six-year-old son was suspended for calling a classmate "poo-poo head." The Texas ACLU also reported that it was challenged at Blessing Elementary School in the Tidehaven Independent School District on grounds that it is "politically, racially or socially offensive." The book was retained.

In the school year 2010–2011, the entire series was challenged at Brookhaven Elementary School in Killeen (Texas) Independent School District because of "sexual content or nudity, offensive to religious sensitivities; use of vulgar terms (fart, burp)."

## AWARDS AND ACCOLADES

One or more of the titles in the series has been named to the following best-seller lists: *USA Today*, Barnes and Noble, *Booksense,* Amazon.com, *New York Times,* and *Publishers Weekly.*

The entire series received the Disney Adventures Kids' Choice Awards in 2007.

*Captain Underpants and the Preposterous Plight of the Purple Potty People*
2009 Garden State Children's Book Award (New Jersey)

*Captain Underpants and the Wrath of the Wicked Wedgie Woman*
2004 Garden State Children's Book Award (New Jersey)
2003 Buckeye Children's Book Award (Ohio)

*Captain Underpants and the Attack of the Talking Toilets*
2002 Garden State Children's Book Award (New Jersey)

*Captain Underpants and the Perilous Plot of Professor Poopypants*
2001 ABC Children's Booksellers Choices Awards

## AUTHOR'S OFFICIAL WEBSITE

www.pilkey.com

**FURTHER READING**

### The Author

Carpenter, Karyn. "Meet Captain Underpants' Creator, Dav Pilkey." *Washington Post,* August 27, 2012. www.washingtonpost.com/ lifestyle/kidspost/meet-dav-pilkeythe-creator-of-captain-underpants/ 2012/08/27/5aa5b2de-ec8a-11e1-a80b-9f898562d0.

"Dav Pilkey." *Contemporary Authors* online, 2010. Books and Authors. Gale.

Lodge, Sally. "Q & A with Dav Pilkey." *Publishers Weekly,* August 5, 2010. www.publishersweekly.com/pw/by-topic/authors/interviews/ article/44061-q-a-with-dav-pilkey.html.

Reid, Rob. "Talking with Dav Pilkey." *Book Links,* a supplement of *Booklist* (June 2011): 18–22.

### The Book

Nissen, Beth. "Captain Underpants: The Straight Poop on a Grossly Entertaining Series of Children's Books." CNN, July 11, 2000. http:// edition.cnn.com/2000/books/news/07/11/captain.underpants.

Roake, Jessica. "One Nation, Underpants: The Triumphant Return of Captain Underpants: Why Kids Love Them, and Parents Should Make Peace with Them." SLATE , September 7, 2012. www.slate .com/articles/arts/family/2012/09/dav_pilkey_s_captain_under pants_books_why_kids_love_them_and_parents_should_make_peace _with_them_.html.

Whelan, Debra Lau. "Dave Pilkey on Captain Underpants #9." *School Library Journal* (September 16, 2012). www.slj.com/2012/09/ authors-illustrators/interviews/interview-dav-pilkey-on-captain -underpants-9/#.

### Censorship

Gibron, Bill. "What's So Funny 'Bout Pee, Poop, and Underwear: The Controversy over *Captain Underpants.*" PopMatters, September 30, 2005. www.popmatters.com/feature/050930-bannedbooks-gibron.

Sauerwein, Kristina. "Irate Grandma Fights 'Captain Underpants.'" *Chicago Tribune,* June 4, 2003. http://articles.chicagotribune.com/ 2003–06–04/news/0306040280_1_deputy-doo-doo-pam-santi-super -diaper-baby.

Trelease, Jim. "Challenging Captain Underpants and the Irrepressible Junie B. Jones." Updated March 30, 2011. www.trelease-on-reading.com/censor7.html#underpants.

### For Listening and Viewing

www.youtube.com/watch?v=jRKQwqfN04A. August 23, 2012. Dav Pilkey talks with a student reporter about his inspiration for the "Captain Underpants" series.

www.youtube.com/watch?v=HY_cMVZITTs. June 24, 2012. Dav Pilkey discusses how "Reading Gives You Superpowers."

www.youtube.com/watch?v=Rrj1Kl-mQJc&list=LP3BE-pnkNtSE&index=2&feature=plcp. June 27, 2011. Dav Pilkey talks about the inspiration for *Super Diaper 2*.

### TALKING WITH READERS ABOUT THE ISSUES

- A lot of kids think "bathroom humor" and "smart-mouthed kids" are really funny. How does the *Captain Underpants* series have both? What else is funny about George and Harold and their superhero, Captain Underpants?
- How does Mr. Krupp change when he becomes Captain Underpants?
- George and Harold misspell a lot of words. Explain how this adds to the humor in the book. How does this fit their character? What kind of grades do you think George and Harold get in English and spelling?
- Some adults don't like the "name-calling" in the books. How is name-calling real in a kid's world? What is the difference between name-calling and bullying? What is the best way to deal with kids who engage in both?
- Another reason that some adults don't like the series is because George and Harold disrespect authority. How do you respond to this complaint? Why is it fun to read about things in books that you may not be allowed to do in real life?

**RELATED BOOKS CHALLENGED FOR SIMILAR REASONS**

*Birdseye, Tom.* **Attack of the Mutant Underwear.** *New York: Holiday House, 2003.*

In 2006 the book was removed from the Pinellas (Florida) Battle of the Books program because officials found it inappropriate for younger readers. At the time the book was on the Sunshine State Young Reader's Award list for third-, fourth-, and fifth-graders.

*Sachar, Louis.* **Wayside School Is Falling Down.** *New York: HarperCollins, 1989.*

In 1995 the book was removed from a suggested reading list from the Antigo elementary reading program in Wisconsin because of passages that "condone destruction of school property, disgraceful manners, disrespectful representation of professionals, improper English, and promotion of peer pressure."

Patricia Polacco

# In Our Mothers' House

*New York: Philomel Books, a division*
*of Penguin Young Readers Group, 2009*

**IT'S RARE THAT A CHILDREN'S PICTURE**
book spans generations, but Patricia
Polacco begins her story when this special family is created and ends the
story with the death of the parents. The parents are a lesbian couple, Marmee and Meema, who want a family so much that they adopt three children.
The oldest, an African American girl, narrates the story. She introduces
readers to her brother Will, an Asian boy adopted at three days old. Then
Millie, a two-month-old redhead, joins the family. The children are happy
with their two mothers, and together they enjoy family gatherings, neighborhood parties, and special holiday traditions. They do encounter one
prejudiced couple that sneers at the family when they see them together,
but for the most part friends and family accept them. The children grow
up, get married, and rear their own children in loving, happy families. The
siblings have such a strong bond that they hold family gatherings in their
mothers' house where Will and his family reside.

*Booklist* (May 1, 2009) states, "Quieter moments radiate the love the
mothers have for their children and for each other." *School Library Journal*
(May 1, 2009) says, "The story serves as a model of inclusiveness." The
reviewer for *The Bulletin of the Center for Children's Books* (July/August
2009) believes that the book is didactic, but states, "children in similar
situations will certainly appreciate seeing their own experiences reflected
in their literature." A reviewer for Rainbowrumpus.org, an online magazine for youth with LGBT parents (accessed December 14, 2012), points
out that the mothers teach their three children to love other people. In
*Library Media Connection* (October 2009), Dennis J. LeLoup calls the book
"a strong and memorable story of a peaceful, devoted family unit."

## CHALLENGES

According to the Texas ACLU 2009–2010 Annual Report, the book was banned from the Intermediate School in Glen Rose, Texas, because of the lesbian couple.

In January 2012 a kindergarten student at the Windridge Elementary School in the Davis County (Utah) School District borrowed *In Our Mothers' House*. The parents issued a formal complaint and soon after, a group of twenty-five parents joined in challenging the book. They claimed that the book "promotes homosexuality" and "violates Utah sex-education laws." The book was placed on a restricted bookshelf, and children must have parental permission to read it. In 2012 a parent of an elementary school child filed a lawsuit against the school district (*Weber v. Davis School District*) claiming that her child's free speech rights had been violated. The courts ruled that children have the right to "choose" their reading materials, and that *In Our Mothers' House* doesn't violate the "sex-education law" since library books aren't considered instructional materials. On January 11, 2013, the Davis School District instructed librarians to return the book to the shelves.

The ALA's Office for Intellectual Freedom recorded one challenge in 2010 and three in 2012, including the challenge in Utah.

## AWARDS AND ACCOLADES

2010 Rainbow Lists

## AUTHOR'S OFFICIAL WEBSITE

www.patriciapolacco.com

## FURTHER READING

### The Author

https://www.scholastic.com/teachers/contributor/patricia-polacco.
Brodie, Carolyn. "Patricia Polacco: Artistic Memories." *School Library Monthly* 14 (June 1998): 44–46.
"Patricia Polacco." *Contemporary Authors* online, 2011. Books and Authors. Gale.

Vandergift, Kay E. "Peacocks, Dreams, Quilds, and Honey: Patricia Polacco, A Woman's Voice of Remembrance." In *Ways of Knowing: Literature and the Intellectual Life of Children*, 259–88. Lanham, MD: Scarecrow, 1996.

## The Book

Thoms, Sue. "Two Moms Create Joyful Home in Patricia Polacco's 'In Our Mothers' House.'" MLive, May 20, 2009. www.mlive.com/living/grand-rapids/index.ssf/2009/05/two_moms_create_joyful_home_in.html.

## Censorship

Block, Joshua. "You Can't Hide Families Behind the Desk: How Utah School Officials Are Violating the First Amendment in Library Book Case." *ACLU Blog,* November 13, 2012. www.aclu.org/blog/lgbt-rights-free-speech/you-cant-hide-families-behind-desk-how-utah-school-officials-are.

Bonner, Johnny. "Utah Parent Sues School over Banned Book." *Courthouse News* (Pasadena, California), November 15, 2012. www.courthousenews.com/2012/11/15/52275.htm.

Francis, JaNae. "Ogden Panel Discusses Censorship of *In Our Mothers' House.*" *Standard Examiner* (Ogden, Utah), June 11, 2012. www.standard.net/stories/2012/06/11/ogden-panel-discusses-censorship-our-mothers-house.

Goldberg, Beverly. "Utah Suit Restores Access to *In Our Mother's House.*" *American Libraries* 45 (March/April 2013): 11.

McEntee, Peg. "McEntee: Nothing to Fear from 'In Our Mother's House.'" *Salt Lake City Tribune,* June 4, 2012. www.sltrib.com/sltrib/news/54239814–78/mcentee-mothers-book-meema.html.csp.

Wood, Benjamin. "ACLU Sues Davis School District over Removal of Book about Family with Same-Sex Parents. *Deseret News* (Salt Lake City), November 13, 2012. www.deseretnews.com/article/865566652/ACLU-sues-Davis-School-District-over-removal-of-book-about-family-with-same-sex-parents.html?pg = all.

## For Listening and Viewing

www.readingrockets.org/books/interviews/polacco. *Reading Rockets.* This is a video interview with Patricia Polacco.

www.youtube.com/watch?v = U8T9LKcaEYo. June 22, 2012. Polacco talks about the censorship issue with *In Our Mothers' House.*

## TALKING WITH READERS ABOUT THE ISSUES

- Talk with children about the meaning of "tolerance" and "diversity."
- Discuss the diversity of the three adopted children in the book. Do they feel different?
- How do their mothers help them celebrate their differences?
- Discuss how the Lockner family reacts to Marmee and Meema and their children. How do the other neighbors show their support?
- Discuss how the mothers teach their children to accept all kinds of people.
- The children are adults at the end of the story. What do you think they tell their children about their two mothers?
- What might we learn about respecting differences from reading *In Our Mothers' House*?

## RELATED BOOKS CHALLENGED FOR SIMILAR REASONS

Freeman, Martha. **The Trouble with Babies.** *Illustrated by Cat Bowman Smith. New York: Holiday House, 2002.*

In the 2010–2011 Texas ACLU Annual Report, this book was challenged at the Jennie Reid Elementary School in the La Porte Independent School District because a gay couple is rearing a child.

Newman, Leslea. **Heather Has Two Mommies.** *Northampton, MA: In Other Words, 1989.*

This book was on the American Library Association's Most Challenged List from 1992 to 1999 because of homosexuality and same-sex parents.

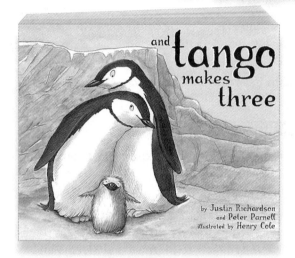

Justin Richardson
and Peter Parnell

## And Tango Makes Three

Illustrated by Henry Cole.
New York: Simon and
Schuster, 2005

ROY AND SILO, TWO INSEPARABLE MALE CHINSTRAP PENGUINS AT THE
Central Park Zoo, imitate the male and female penguin couples by building their own nest. When Roy notices a stone that resembles an egg, he
places it in the nest and the two care for it in the same loving way as the
other penguins tend to their eggs. Chicks are hatched, and Roy and Silo
are puzzled that nothing is happening with their stone egg. Mr. Gramzay,
the zookeeper, notices their behavior and decides to give them an egg
that other penguins couldn't care for. When they successfully hatch the
egg, Mr. Gramzay names the chick Tango "because it takes two to make a
Tango." Roy and Silo nurture Tango by feeding her, snuggling with her in
their nest, and taking her for a swim with the other penguin families. Soon
after Tango was born, the penguin house became a popular place to visit
at the zoo because families wanted to see little Tango and her two daddies.
In the "Author's Note," Richardson and Parnell state, "After years of living
side by side in the Central Park Zoo, they (Roy and Silo) discovered each
other in 1998 and they have been a couple ever since."

Julia Roach, reviewer for *School Library Journal* (July 1, 2005), writes,
"This joyful story about the meaning of family is a must for any library."
*Publishers Weekly* (May 16, 2005) states that the book can "serve as a
gentle jumping-off point for discussions about same-sex partnerships."
The reviewer for *Kirkus* (June 1, 2005) applauds "the theme of acceptance." And they believe that it is done in a "non-preachy way." In her
review in *Booklist* (May 15, 2005), Jennifer Mattson writes that readers

will return to the book many times because of the "celebration of patient, loving fathers who 'knew just what to do.'" Karen Breen states on her blog, BreeniBooks (February 4, 2008), "Roy and Silo have so much to teach about love and life."

Since this is a true story, it was originally published and classified as nonfiction. In a later printing, it was reclassified as a picture book because the publisher felt that would give children greater access to the book. Some libraries have continued to shelve the book as nonfiction with the idea that it won't be as accessible to young children.

## CHALLENGES

The book was the American Library Association's Most Challenged Book in 2006, 2007, 2008, and 2010. It was the second Most Challenged in 2009. It has been challenged in public and school libraries, and in some cases, removed or placed on a restricted shelf.

The book was challenged in 2006 at the Shiloh Elementary School library in Illinois. A committee of school employees and a parent suggested that the book be moved to a separate shelf, requiring parent permission before checkout. The school superintendent rejected the proposal and the book remained on the library shelf.

In a May 8, 2007, *School Library Journal* blog article, the librarian at Woodland Elementary in Southwick, Massachusetts, discusses her fear of losing her job when in her absence a substitute teacher took issue with the content of the book and took a copy to the administrator. The book was being used with second graders in a unit about "All Kinds of Families." There was no formal complaint filed by the substitute, but the administration wrote a threatening letter to the librarian. The issue was eventually resolved.

In 2007 the book was removed from four elementary school libraries in Charlotte-Mecklenburg, North Carolina, after a few parents and a county commissioner raised questions about the content. It should be noted that no formal challenge was issued. The book was returned to the shelves after a local newspaper questioned the ban.

The book was challenged in 2008 in Loudoun County, Virginia, but was returned to the sixteen elementary school libraries despite the complaint about its subject matter. It was also challenged but retained in 2008 at the

Eli Pinney Elementary School in Dublin, Ohio, despite a parent's concern that the book "is based on one of those subjects that is best left to be discovered by students at another time or in another place." Other challenges in 2008 occurred in Ankeny, Iowa, where the school board voted six to one to retain the book even though parents felt the book promotes homosexuality; Calvert County Library in Prince Frederick, Maryland, where a formal request to remove the book from the children's section and shelve it in a labeled alternative section failed.

In 2009 it was challenged but retained in the North Kansas, Missouri City schools despite a parent's concern that the book wasn't age-appropriate, didn't follow the district's policy on human sexuality education, and tries to indoctrinate children about homosexuality. It was also challenged but retained in the Meadowview Elementary School in Farmington, Minnesota, despite a parent's concern that "a topic such as sexual preference does not belong in a library where it can be obtained by young elementary students." It was also banned in all elementary schools in the Northside Independent School District in Texas because it is "politically, racially, or socially offensive." In the same year, it was challenged at all elementary schools in the Midway Independent School District in Texas. It was retained, but restricted. It was simply deemed "not age appropriate."

In 2011 the book was pulled from the Gibbs Elementary School in Rochester, Minnesota, as inappropriate for elementary school students and removed from the school library shelves. The decision was later reversed as a mistake for failing to follow district policy. A "temporary resolution" requires one of the parents who challenged the book be present when their child checks out the book.

*Blogging Censorship,* the official blog of the National Coalition Against Censorship (NCAC) provides an analysis of the challenges to *And Tango Makes Three* in an August 5, 2011, entry. NCAC conducted a short survey of fifty-nine people about the book's content and its age-appropriateness. Eighty-six percent "felt comfortable with this book being available to children. A summary of the book's controversy states that it "encourages homosexuality."

Additional challenges have been recorded in California, Georgia, Indiana, Missouri, and Wisconsin.

## AWARDS AND ACCOLADES

2006  American Library Association Notable Children's Book
2006  Bank Street Best Book of the Year
2006  Cooperative Children's Book Center, University of Wisconsin Choice
2006  Children's Book Council and National Council for Social Studies Notable Book
2006  American Society for the Prevention of Cruelty to Animals (ASCPA) Henry Bergh Award
2006  Gustavus Myer Award
2006  Lambda Literary Award Finalist

## FURTHER READING

### The Authors

Bowllan Amy. "Meet Peter Parnell and Justin Richardson, Authors of *And Tango Makes Three.*" Bowllan's Blog, *School Library Journal* (January, 26, 2007). http://blogs.slj.com/bowllansblog/2007/01/26/meet-peter-parnell-and-justin-richardson-authors-of-and-tango-makes-three-2.

### The Book

Magmuson, Marta L. "Perceptions of Self and the 'Other': An Analysis of Challenges to *And Tango Makes Three.*" *School Library Media Research* 14 (January 2011): 4.

Smith, Dinita, "Love That Dare Not Squeak Its Name. *New York Times,* February 7, 2004. www.nytimes.com/2004/02/07/arts/love-that-dare-not-squeak-its-name.html.

### Censorship

Chandler, Michael Alison. "2 Guys and a Chick Set Off Loudoun Library Dispute." *Washington Post,* February 17, 2008. www.washingtonpost.com/wp-dyn/content/article/2008/02/16/AR2008021600749.html.

Daniel, Corey. "*And Tango Makes Three*, a Banned Book That Can Make a Difference." Examiner (Winston-Salem), June 20, 2012. www

.examiner.com/article/and-tango-makes-three-a-banned-book-that
-can-make-*a-difference.*

Johnson, Jenna and Christy Goodman, "Library Backs Book on Same-Sex
Parents." *Washington Post,* October 23, 2009. www.washingtonpost
.com/wp-dyn/content/article/2008/10/22/AR2008102200196
.html?nav = rss_education.

Stolle, Matthew, "Superintendent: Book Was Pulled from School Library
in Error." *The Post Bulletin* (Rochester, Minnesota), March 19, 2012;
updated March 20, 2012. www.postbulletin.com/news/local/
superintendent-book-was-pulled-from-school-library-in-error/
article_1756c45c-f8bd-59cc-a181-dfd2081297a2.html.

Suhr, Jim. "Parents Want Gay Books Blocked." *Washington Post,* November 16, 2006. www.washingtonpost.com/wp-dyn/content/article/
2006/11/16/AR2006111602008_pf.html.

## For Listening and Viewing

www.youtube.com/watch?v = L-8ehpyDwRA. Peter Parnell and Justin
Richardson read from *And Tango Makes Three.*

www.teachingbooks.net/book_reading.cgi?id = 5645&a = 1. Justin Richardson discusses *And Tango Makes Three* and reads from the book.

## TALKING WITH READERS ABOUT THE ISSUES

- What is the definition of family? Compare and contrast Tango's
family to the other penguin families in the zoo.
- Why does Mr. Gramzay, the zookeeper, give Roy and Silo an egg?
How does he know that Roy and Silo love one another?
- How are Roy and Silo good parents?
- What makes Tango so special?
- What can we learn about family, love, and differences from Tango's
story?

## RELATED BOOKS CHALLENGED FOR SIMILAR REASONS

Brown, Marc. **Buster's Sugartime.** *New York: Little, Brown Books for Young Readers, a division of Hachette Book Group, 2006.*

In 2009 this book was challenged, but retained at the Union District elementary school libraries in Oklahoma despite a parent's complaint that the book features two same-sex couples and their children.

Willhoite, Michael. **Daddy's Roommate.** *Boston: Alyson Books, 1991.*

This is one of the most challenged books from 1992 to 2000 because of homosexuality and same-sex parents.

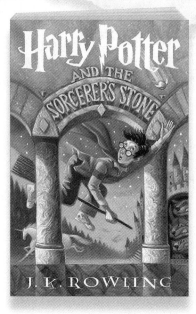

*J. K. Rowling*

# Harry Potter series

*New York: Scholastic, 1977–2007*

HARRY POTTER, AN ORPHAN, WAS ONLY an infant when he was dropped on the doorsteps of an aunt and uncle, the Dursleys. It turns out that the Dursleys are muggles (non-magical) and they treat Harry dreadfully and force him to sleep in a cupboard below the stairs. In the first book of the series, *Harry Potter and the Sorcerer's Stone,* Harry receives a visit on his eleventh birthday from Hagrid, a giant, who grants him an invitation to attend the Hogwarts School of Witchcraft and Wizardry. There he discovers that he is a wizard and has the special powers to combat the evil Voldemort, his parents' murderer. Harry makes it through his first year at Hogwarts and along the way makes friends, and a few enemies. In *Harry Potter and the Chamber of Secrets*, the second book, Harry is on summer break from Hogwarts School and back at the Dursleys. Harry heeds a warning from a house-elf that he is in danger. Three classmates from Hogwarts rescue him, and the four set out to solve the mystery of the Chamber of Secrets. There's a rumor circulating that Harry is an heir of Slytherin, one of the school's founders. This puts Harry in a precarious situation with his friends, and he must go alone to the bottom of the Chamber of Secrets and fight the giant serpent.

Each book in the series chronicles one year in Harry's life at Hogwarts. He deals with the usual adolescent issues, but he always has new dangers to face and new mysteries to solve. He continues to collect new friends, and enemies, and with the help of his special powers he finds that he can face both the good and evil that come his way. In the seventh and final book, *Harry Potter and the Deathly Hallows*, Harry turns seventeen and engages in a final dual with Voldmort, who becomes victim of his own curse and dies.

In the "Epilogue," Harry and Ginny Weasley are married and the parents of three children. One of the sons is about to follow in his father's footsteps and attend Hogwarts. The boy experiences apprehensions but he has one person pulling for him—his father.

*Horn Book Magazine* (January 1, 1999) calls *Harry Potter and the Sorcerer's Stone* "a charming and readable romp." Michael Cart, reviewer for *Booklist* (September 15, 1998) says this first book is "brilliantly imagined and beautifully written."

*Kirkus* (June 1, 1999) says, "Harry steadily rises to every challenge" in the second book of the series, *Harry Potter and the Chamber of Secrets*. *School Library Journal* (July 1999) points out the "sly and sophisticated humor" of the second book. And *Voice of Youth Advocates* (August 1, 1999) praises the "blend of humor and fantasy."

*Harry Potter and the Prisoner of Azkaban* received rave reviews. *Publishers Weekly* (July 19, 1999) says the book shows "the genius of Rowling's plotting." *Horn Book Magazine* (December 1, 1999) calls it "quite a good book." The reviewer for *Voice of Youth Advocates* (December 1, 1999) states, "character development is stronger in this book." And *School Library Journal* (September 1, 1999) says "some things get better and better."

*Publishers Weekly* (July 17, 2000) reviews the 752-page *Harry Potter and the Goblet of Fire* and states that the "climax is more spectacular" than the first three books. *Booklist* (August 10, 2000) says the "magic becomes more embellished and layered." And *School Library Journal* (August 1, 2000) praises the "imagination, humor and suspense."

Ilene Cooper reviews *Harry Potter and the Order of the Phoenix* for *Booklist* (July 1, 2003) and says, "You can't put it down." The reviewer for *School Library Journal* (August 1, 2003) says there is something for everyone in the book, "magic" for children, and "coming of age" issues for young adults.

The *Booklist* (August 1, 2005) review of *Harry Potter and the Half-Blood Prince* says, "Rowling is at the top of her game here." *School Library Journal* (September 1, 2005) recommends the books for grades 5–up and calls it "darker and more difficult" than the earlier works.

In the *Publishers Weekly* (July 30, 2007) review of *Harry Potter and the Deathly Hallows*, the reviewer states that Rowling ends the series in an "old-fashioned way, without ambiguity."

## The Books

*Harry Potter and the Sorcerer's Stone* (1997)
  British title: *Harry Potter and the Philosopher's Stone*
*Harry Potter and the Chamber of Secrets* (1999)
*Harry Potter and the Prisoner of Azkaban* (1999)
*Harry Potter and the Goblet of Fire* (2000)
*Harry Potter and the Order of the Phoenix* (2003)
*Harry Potter and the Half-Blood Prince* (2005)
*Harry Potter and the Deathly Hallows* (2007)

## CHALLENGES

It should be noted that in 2002, a federal judge overturned restricted access to the *Harry Potter* books after parents of a Cedarville, Arkansas, fourth-grader filed a federal lawsuit challenging the restrictions, which required students to present written permission from a parent to borrow a book.

The *Harry Potter* books were #1 on the American Library Association's Top 100 Challenged Books List: 2000–2009. They were #1 on the Top Ten Most Challenged in 2001 and 2002.

In 1999 *Harry Potter and the Sorcerer's Stone, Harry Potter and the Chamber of Secrets,* and *Harry Potter and the Prisoner of Azkaban* were challenged in South Carolina schools because the books have a "serious tone of death, hate, lack of respect, and sheer evil."

In 2000, all three books were challenged, but retained in the Arab, Alabama, school libraries and Accelerated Reader program over objections that the author "is a member of the occult and the book encourages children to practice witchcraft." In the same year, the novels were challenged, but retained in the Frankfort (Illinois) School District 157-C because parents were concerned that the book contains "lying and smart-aleck retorts to adults." The books were also restricted to fifth- through eighth-graders who have written parent permission in the Zeeland, Minnesota, school. The administration issued an order that no further books in the series be purchased and teachers are prohibited from reading the book aloud in class. The book was considered objectionable because of the "intense story line, the violence, the wizardry, and the sucking of animal blood." The three books were restricted in the Santa Fe (Texas) School District because of "witchcraft." In 2002 there was a proposal to remove these three books, along with more that fifty other titles, by a teachers' prayer group at the high school in Russell Springs, Kentucky, because the books deal with "ghosts, cults, and witchcraft."

In 2001 the three books, along with *Harry Potter and the Goblet of Fire*, were burned outside Christ Community Church in Alamagordo, New Mexico, because the *Potter* series is "a masterpiece of satanic deception." In the same year, all four books were challenged in the Owen J. Roberts School District classrooms in Bucktown, Pennsylvania, because the books tell children that "lying, cheating, and stealing are not only acceptable, but they are cool and cute."

A parent's plea to take the series out of the Gwinnett County Schools in Georgia failed in 2006. *Harry Potter and the Half-Blood Prince* was removed in 2006 by the Wilsona School District trustees from a list recommended by a parent-teacher for the Vista San Gabriel Elementary School library in Palmdale, California. Twenty-three other books were also removed.

In 2007 the entire *Harry Potter* series was removed from the St. Joseph School in Wakefield, Massachusetts, because the themes of "witchcraft and sorcery" were inappropriate for a Catholic school.

## AWARDS AND ACCOLADES

2008 Mythopoeic Fantasy Award for Children's Literature
2007 NEA Teachers' Top 100 Books for Children
2000 J. K. Rowling named Author of the Year in the United Kingdom

### *Harry Potter and the Sorcerer's Stone*

2001 Louisiana Young Readers Choice Award
2001 Rebecca Caudill Young Reader' Choice Book Award (Illinois)
2001 South Carolina Book Awards: Junior Books
2001 West Virginia Children's Choice Book Award
2000 Blue Hen Book Award: Chapter Book (Delaware)
2000 Charlotte Award: Young Adult (New York)
2000 Golden Archer Book Award: Middle/Junior (Wisconsin)
2000 Grand Canyon Reader Award: Teen Book (Arizona)
2000 Great Stone Face Children's Book Award (New Hampshire)
2000 Indian Paintbrush Book Award (Wyoming)
2000 Massachusetts Children's Book Award
2000 Nene Book Award (Hawaii)
1999 ABC Children's Booksellers Choice Awards

1999  E. B. White Read-Aloud Awards: Middle Reader
1998  *Booklist* Editors' Choice
1998  *School Library Journal* Best Books

### Harry Potter and the Chamber of Secrets

2003  Blue Spruce Young Adult Book Award (Colorado)
2000  Galaxy British Book Awards
2000  ALA/ALSC Notable Books for Children List
2000  ALA/YALSA Best Books List
1999  *New York Times* Notable Book
1999  *Publishers Weekly* Best Book of the Year
1999  *School Library Journal* Best Book of the Year

### Harry Potter and the Goblet of Fire

2002  Golden Archer
2002  Indian Paintbrush Book Award (Wyoming)
2001  ALA/ALSC Notable Children's Books
2001  ABC Children's Bestsellers Choices Award

### Harry Potter and the Prisoner of Azkaban

2004  Blue Spruce Young Adult Book Award (Colorado)
2004  Indian Paintbrush Book Award (Wyoming)
2000  ALA/ALSC Notable Children's Books List
2000  ALA/YALSA Best Books List
2001  Golden Archer Awards: Intermediate (Wisconsin)
2001  Maine Student Book Award
1999  *Booklist* Editors' Choice: Books for Youth: Middle Readers
      Category

### Harry Potter and the Order of the Phoenix

2006  Blue Spruce Young Adult Book Awards (Colorado)
2005  Golden Archer Awards: Middle/Junior High School (Wisconsin)
2004  ALA/ALSC Notable Children's Books List
2005  ALA/YALSA Best Books List
2003  *Booklist* Editors' Choice: Books for Youth: Middle Readers
      Category

### Harry Potter and the Half-Blood Prince

2008   Blue Spruce Book Award for Young Adults (Colorado)
2006   ALA/YALSA Best Books List
2005   Golden Archer Awards: Middle/Junior High School (Wisconsin)
2005   *New York Times* Notable Books: Children's Books
2005   *Booklist* Editors' Choice: Older Readers

### Harry Potter and the Deathly Hallows

2008   ALA/ALSC Notable Children's Books List
2008   ALA/YALSA Best Books List
2008   USBBY Outstanding International Books: Grades 6–8
2007   *Booklist* Editors' Choice: Books for Youth: Older Readers Category
2007   *New York Times* Notable Books: Children's Books

## AUTHOR'S OFFICIAL WEBSITE

www.jkrowling.com/en_US

## PUBLISHER'S OFFICIAL HARRY POTTER WEBSITE

http://harrypotter.scholastic.com

## FURTHER READING

### The Author

Grosman, Lev. "J. K. Rowling Hogwarts and All." *Time* 166 (July 25, 2005): 60–65.

"J. K. Rowling." *Contemporary Authors* online, 2014. Books and Authors. Gale.

MacDonald, Joan Vos. *J. K. Rowling*. Berkeley Heights, NJ: Enslow, 2008. 104 p. (Authors Teens Love Series)

MacDonald, Joan Vos. *J. K. Rowling: Banned, Challenged and Censored*. Berkley Heights, NJ: Enslow, 2008. 160 p. (Authors of Banned Books Series)

Shapiro, Marc. *J. K. Rowling: The Wizard Behind Harry*. St. Martin's/Griffin, an imprint of Macmillan, 2000. 240 p.

Sickels, Amy. *The Mythmaker: The Story of J. K. Rowling.* New York: Facts on File, 2008. 136 p. (Who Wrote That? Series)

## The Books

Black, Sharon. "The Magic of Harry Potter: The Symbols and Heroes of Fantasy." *Children's Literature in Education* 34 (September 2003): 237–47.

Byam, Paige. "Children's Literature or Adult Classic? The *Harry Potter* series and the British Novel Tradition." *Washington Jefferson College Review* 54 (Fall 2004): 7–13.

Feldman, Roxanne, and J. K. Rowling. "The Truth about Harry." *School Library Journal* 45, no. 9 (September 1999): 136–39.

Hallet, Vicky. "The Power of Potter." *U.S. News and World Report* 139 (July 25, 2005): 45–51.

Knapp, Nancy Flanagan. "In Defense of Harry Potter: An Apologia." *School Libraries Worldwide* 9 (January 2003): 78–91.

Opar, Tamara. "Why Do Children Love Harry Potter?" *Journal of Youth Services* in Libraries 15 (September 2002): 32–33.

Tucker, Nicholas. "The Rise and Rise of Harry Potter." *Children's Literature* in Education 30 (December 1999): 221–34.

## Censorship

Blume, Judy. "Is Harry Potter Evil?" *New York Times*, October 22, 1999. www.nytimes.com/1999/10/22/opinion/is-harry-potter-evil.html.

Denton, Peter H. "What Could Be Wrong with Harry?" *Journal of Youth Services in Libraries* 15 (Spring 202): 28–32.

Gish, Kimbra Wilder. "Hunting Down Harry Potter: An Exploration of Religious Concerns about Children's Literature." *Horn Book Magazine* 76 (May/June 2000): 262–71.

Seufert, Carmelita. "Burned and Banned." *Read* 56 (September 25, 2006): 14–17.

Zimmereman, Jonathan. "Harry Potter and His Censors." *Education Week* 19 (August 2, 2000): 44.

## For Listening and Viewing

www.youtube.com/watch?v = Uv106JJMC50. July 24, 2013. J. K.
   Rowling interviews with Oprah Winfrey.

www.youtube.com/watch?v = CQAvoiTVyHo. August 27, 2013.
   J. K. Rowling speaks about the fifteenth anniversary of the publication of the first Harry Potter book in the United States.

## TALKING WITH READERS ABOUT THE ISSUES

- Define fantasy. How do the *Harry Potter* books fit the elements of
  fantasy?
- Susan Cooper, author of *The Dark Is Rising* series, believes that fantasy challenges a reader to think more deeply about themes. What
  are the underlying themes in the *Harry Potter* books? Explain how
  these themes connect to the reality of one's world.
- The *Harry Potter* books are among the most censored books in the
  United States. Those who oppose the books call them "evil" and
  believe that they promote an interest in the "occult." Identify the
  "good" and "evil" forces in the book. What "Talking Points" might
  you use to defend the *Harry Potter* books to the critics?
- Debate the claim that the *Harry Potter* books confuse readers about
  religion.
- The *Harry Potter* books have been banned in school and public
  libraries, and a few churches have actually burned the books in
  a bonfire before entire congregations and the media. How does
  banning a book create more interest in reading it? Discuss why one
  person or group doesn't have the right to control what others read.

## RELATED NOVELS CHALLENGED FOR SIMILAR REASONS

*Alexander, Lloyd.* **The Chronicles of Prydain,** *a series of five fantasy novels.*
*New York: Holt, an imprint of Macmillan, 1964–1968.*

This entire series was challenged as required reading at the North Bridge
Middle School in Massachusetts in 1993 because the novels "contain religious themes that are pagan in nature and young minds would be drawn
to the allure of witchcraft and black magic."

*Clapp, Patricia.* **Witches' Children.** *New York: Puffin paperbacks, an imprint
    of Penguin Random House, 1987.*

In 1991 the book was challenged at the Howard County schools in Maryland because it was "not appropriate positive pleasurable reading for the
young age group." It was also challenged in 1990 at the Cannon Road Elementary School library in Silver Spring, Maryland, because students who
read it will be encouraged "to dabble in the occult."

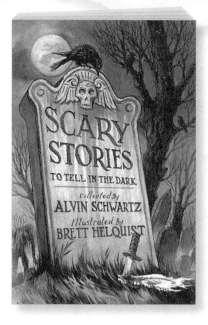

*Alvin Schwartz*

# Scary Stories series

*New York: HarperCollins, 1981–1991; illustrated by Stephen Gammell. New editions, 2010–2011; illustrated by Brett Helquist*

**THE THREE BOOKS IN THE *SCARY STORIES*** series draw on folklore—old tales and urban legends—as the basis for ghost stories, verses, and songs that send chills down the spine. *Scary Stories to Tell in the Dark* includes chilling stories like "The Big Toe" and "The Ghost with Bloody Finders"; *More Scary Stories to Tell in the Dark* sends readers screaming with horror and delight with tales like "A Weird Blue Light" and "Cemetery Soup"; and *Scary Stories 3: More Tales to Chill Your Bones* anthologizes tales of terror like "Footsteps" and "Is Something Wrong?" Since most of the tales originated from the oral tradition, storytellers often use them. For those who are learning the art of storytelling, Schwartz includes tips for telling: "As you shout the last words, stamp your foot and jump at someone nearby." Many of the stories have a perfect logical or humorous ending; others have an ending that can only be explained through the supernatural. In the earlier editions, Stephen Gammell's black-and-white illustrations, liberally scattered throughout all three books, have the right balance of realism and malevolence to sustain the books' eerie tone. The books were reissued with new and toned-down illustrations which brought criticism from some critics.

The first book contains six pages of source notes for the tales and a bibliography that includes both the sources and books for further reading. In the two sequels, the notes and source information are even more detailed.

The reviewer for *Kirkus* (October 1, 1982) states that the tales in *Scary Stories to Tell in the Dark* are "all perfectly tailored for reading aloud."

*School Library Journal* (January 1982) calls the stories "unusually good" and "not unbearably grotesque."

*School Library Journal* (February 1985) says that *More Scary Stories to Tell in the Dark* is "a book guaranteed to make your teeth chatter." The reviewer also writes, "Gammell's illustrations give realistic definition to the ghouls." Martha V. Parravano reviewed the new edition of *More Scary Stories to Tell in the Dark* for *The Horn Book Guide* (Spring 2011) and calls Brett Helquist's illustrations "altogether more benign than the nightmarish Stephen Gammell's originals."

*Horn Book Magazine* (November/December 1991) calls *Scary Stories 3: More Tales to Chill Your Bones* "enticing" and states, "The anecdotal tone suggests that these unnerving events just might have happened." *School Library Journal* (November 1991) says that readers are called upon to "put their imaginative skills to full use."

## CHALLENGES

According to data collected by the ALA's Office for Intellectual Freedom, the entire series was #1 on the Top 100 Most Frequently Challenged Books: 1990–1999. The series was #7 on the Top 100 Banned/Challenged Books List: 2000–2009. In 2012 the series was #8 on the Top Ten Most Challenged Books because of "violence" and "unsuited to age group." The series was #4 on the Top Ten Most Challenged Books List in 2008. Reasons cited were "occult/Satanism and religious viewpoint." In 2006 the series was #6 on the Top Ten Most Challenged Books List for "insensitivity, occult/Satanism/, and unsuited to age group."

The entire series was challenged at the Lake Washington School District in Kirkland, Washington, in 1992 as "unacceptably violent for children." In 1994 all three books were removed from the Vancouver (Washington) School District libraries after surviving two previous attempts in 1991 and 1993. They were also challenged at the neighboring Evergreen School District libraries in Vancouver because the books are "far beyond other scary books." In 1993 the three books were challenged in Columbus, Ohio, because children shouldn't be "scared by materials that they read in schools."

*Scary Stories to Tell in the Dark* and *Scary Stories 3: More Tales to Chill Your Bones* were challenged in 1992 at the West Hartford, Connecticut, elementary and middle school libraries because of "violence and the subject matter."

*Scary Stories to Tell in the Dark* and *More Scary Stories to Tell in the Dark* were challenged at the Neely Elementary School in Gilbert, Arizona, in 1992 because the books show "the dark side of religion through the occult, the devil, and Satanism."

The first book, *Scary Stories to Tell in the Dark,* was restricted to students in the fourth grade or higher in all Enfield, Connecticut, elementary school libraries in 1992. It was challenged by a parent of a student at Happy Valley Elementary School in Glasgow, Kentucky, in 1993 because the book was "too scary." In the same year, the book was restricted at the Marana (Arizona) Unified School District because of complaints about "violence and cannibalism." There have been additional challenges in Indiana, Michigan, and Washington.

*More Scary Stories to Tell in the Dark* was restricted at the Marana (Arizona) Unified School District in 1993 because of "complaints about violence and cannibalism." It was unsuccessfully challenged at the Whittier Elementary School Library in Bozeman, Montana, in 1994 on the ground it would cause children to fear the dark and have nightmares, and would give them an unrealistic view of death.

It was also challenged, but retained on a district reading list in Harper Woods, Michigan, in 1995. The Texas ACLU reports the following challenges: in 2002–2003 at Ellis Elementary School in the Arlington Independent School District for "violence or horror, mysticism or paganism;" 2010–2011, challenged, but retained at Union Hill Elementary School in the Round Rock Independent School District because of "horror;" and in 2012–2013, challenged, but retained at Friendship Elementary School in the Keller Independent School District because of "violence and horror."

## AWARDS AND ACCOLADES

### Scary Stories to Tell in the Dark

    1987  Buckeye Children's Book Award (Ohio)
    1987  Grand Canyon Children's Book Award (Arizona)

### More Scary Stories to Tell in the Dark

    1989 Buckeye Children's Book Award (Ohio)

### Scary Stories 3: More Tales to Chill Your Bones

    1993  Buckeye Children's Book Award (Ohio)

## FURTHER READING

### The Author/Illustrator

"Alvin Schwartz." *Contemporary Authors* online, 2000. Detroit: Gale. Biography in Context. April 2, 2014.

"Alvin Schwartz." *Major Authors and Illustrators for Children and Young Adults.* Detroit: Gale, 2002. Biography in Context. April 2, 2014.

Marcus, Leonard. "Night Visions: Conversations with Alvin Schwartz and Judith Gorog." *The Lion and the Unicorn* 12 (June 1988): 44–62.

"Stephen Gammell." *Contemporary Authors* online, 2007. Books and Authors. Gale.

Vardell, Sylvia. "Profile: Alvin Schwartz." *Language Arts* 64, no. 4 (April 1987): 426–32.

### The Books

Childs, Brian. "Scary Stories to Tell in the Dark: The Terrifying Children's Illustrations of Stephen Gammell." *Comics Alliance,* October 25, 2010. http://comicsalliance.com/scary-stories-to-tell-in-the-dark-art.

Jones, Patrick. "Have No Fear: Scary Stories for the Middle Grades." *Emergency Librarians* 21 (September/October 1993): 30–32.

Schwartz, Alvin. "Children, Humor and Folklore." *Catholic World* 59 (September/October 1987): 67–70.

### Censorship

Blades, John. "Who Is Alvin Schwartz and Why Do Parents Want to Ban His Books." *Chicago Tribune,* September 20, 1993. http://articles .chicagotribune.com/1993–09–20/features/9309200016_1_alvin -schwartz-scary-stories-stephen-gammell.

### For Listening and Viewing

www.youtube.com/watch?v = MvbU1dOz_1c. This is the complete audiobook of *Scary Stories to Tell in the Dark.*

www.youtube.com/watch?v = k-E2ZlqCThA. This is the complete audio-book of *More Scary Stories to Tell in the Dark.*

www.youtube.com/watch?v = qDmce0e0ce4. This is the complete audio-book of *Scary Stories 3: More Tales to Chill Your Bones.*

## TALKING WITH READERS ABOUT THE ISSUES

- Define folklore. Why are ghost stories considered folklore? Many of the stories have been passed down through generations of storytellers. How might storytellers make the stories more or less scary with each telling?
- The *Scary Stories* series has been banned and challenged in some elementary schools because they are considered "too scary." What is the appeal of scary stories? Compare and contrast the scary elements in Schwartz's stories and fairy tales like *Little Red Riding Hood*.
- Stephen Gammell illustrated the first editions of the Scary Stories series. The volumes were reissued in 2010 and 2011 with new illustrations. Some critics feel that the new illustrations aren't as eerie as Gammell's. Debate the possibility that the illustrations were changed to tone down the horror of the stories. Why is it important for the illustrations to reflect the tone of the texts?
- The books have been challenged because they "might give children nightmares" and "children shouldn't be scared by materials they read in schools." Discuss whether the books should be banned from all readers because a few may be frightened.
- The series has also been challenged for "violence." What is the difference between "violence" and "horror"? Which stories might critics label "violent"? These same critics feel that the books are "unsuited for age group." Why is it difficult to assign an age group to any type of folklore?

## RELATED BOOKS CHALLENGED FOR SIMILAR REASONS

*Parvis, Sarah.* **Creepy Castles.** *New York: Bearport, 2008.*

This book was banned from the Clements/Parsons Elementary School in the Copperas Cove Independent School District in Texas because of "violence or horror."

*Stamper, J. P.* **More Tales for the Midnight Hour.** *New York: Scholastic, 1992.*

In 1992 this book was challenged at the Neely Elementary School in Gilbert, Arizona, because it shows the "dark side of religion through the occult, the devil, and satanism."

*Adam Selzer*

# How to Get Suspended and Influence People

*New York: Delacorte, an imprint of Penguin Random House, 2007*

**LEON IS FOURTEEN YEARS OLD AND IN THE** eighth grade when his "gifted and talented" class is given the assignment to make some type of educational video for sixth and seventh graders. The teacher circulates a list of suggested topics and instructs the students to discuss their chosen topic and conduct research that supports the facts before they begin filming. Leon is surprised that sex education is one of the topics, and decides that he can make a much more informative and entertaining film than the ones that he has been shown in class. His thought is that no kid wants to see a "lame video" with "line drawings of private parts." The wheels begin turning inside his head, and he thinks if his film is "artsy" enough that he can get by with including what kids really want to know. He knows from experience that kids don't want to see a film about how normal they are. Instead they want to know things like "how big things should be at a certain age." Can he get his idea past the teacher? Will they try to censor his film? Leon understands enough about his school to know that it's a real possibility that he won't get a favorable response. But he has studied the U.S. Constitution in social studies and he is quite certain that he is protected under the First Amendment.

Mrs. Smollet, the director of the gifted program, disapproves of Leon's film and sees that he is suspended. She thinks that Leon's parents are terrible role models, and feels that having to work with kids like Leon creates a "hostile work environment" for a fine Christian lady like herself. Leon is an overnight success in the eyes of the students. Even kids who think he is a "nerd," and ones who have bullied him in the past are on his side. They line the halls and chant, "Free Leon." Even Coach Wilkins informs students that Leon is a "political prisoner" and encourages them to support him. Leon views his film, titled *La Dolce Pubert,* a success because almost all the kids eventually see it. A classmate posted it on the Internet, and students passed around copies to one another. "Lots of the younger kids thought it great, mostly because it showed some naked paintings and used the word 'whacking' several times." And it made sex education far more interesting.

Jennifer Mattson, a reviewer for *Booklist* (January 1, 2007), states, "Many creative young readers—perhaps especially those who identify with 'miscreant' kids . . . will appreciate and applaud Leon's commitment to his quirky vision." The *Kirkus* (February 1, 2007) reviewer says, "There's definite appeal in the 'kid-wins-over teacher' plot." *Publishers Weekly* (February 26, 2007) states that there are kids who will "empathize with Leon's attitude toward school." The reviewer for *Voice of Youth Advocates* (April 1, 2007) isn't enthusiastic about the book, but does believe it may appeal to those who want "information about sexuality." Pat Scales, reviewer for *School Library Journal* (March 1, 2007), calls the novel "funny and fast-paced," and points out that it may teach "a lesson or two about free speech as well."

" I've dealt with the sort of people who want to ban books all my life. Book-banning was sort of a popular sport in the town where I went to high school. I felt as though the books they chose to go after were usually just random picks that they could use to set a precedent, so they could go after every other book that didn't fit in with their idea of values. I have plenty of books that they'd probably like even less if they actually read them!"

—Adam Selzer, author of *How to Get Suspended and Influence People*

**CHALLENGES**

In 2009 Selzer's novel was challenged at the Nampa Public Library in Idaho by a parent "appalled that the cover included an abstract drawing of a nude woman and the back cover contains some profanity." It's worth noting that the parent challenged the book not for content, but for the information on the cover.

## AUTHOR'S OFFICIAL WEBSITE

www.adamselzer.com

## FURTHER READING

### The Author

"Adam Selzer." *Contemporary Authors* online, 2008. Books and Authors. Gale.

### Censorship

Henninger, Susan. "Banned: 2 Authors of Teen Books Discuss Book Banning and Liberating Literature." *Genesee Valley and Rochester Area Parent*, September 2009. www.gvparent.com/articles/1/09 -banned-book.
Selzer, Adam. "On Censorship." www.adamselzer.com/2008_09_01 _archive.html.

### For Listening and Viewing

www.youtube.com/watch?v = bE7bMbDO_9c. September 17, 2010. This is a live news story about the challenge to the novel in Idaho.
www.kboi2.com/news/local/65713872.html. October 23, 2009. This local Idaho CBS affiliate features the challenge to Selzer's novel at the Nampa Public Library.

## TALKING WITH READERS ABOUT THE ISSUES

- The students at school stand up for Leon when he is suspended. Leon says, "They weren't protesting for me, they were protesting against school." Discuss what the students learned about "free speech" and their school by engaging in a protest.
- Why is Coach Wilkins on Leon's side? Explain why he tries to rally the entire faculty around Leon.

- In reference to Mrs. Smollet, the principal says to Leon, "There's a fine line between monitoring students' behavior and pushing your own agenda, and sometimes it gets a little blurry." What agenda is Mrs. Smollet pushing? Debate whether the principal's statement signals a victory for Leon and the students.
- Explain why Leon thinks that getting banned was the best thing that happened to his film.
- Leon says that Anna is the first kid he had ever known who refused to pledge allegiance to the flag. Why is he intrigued with Anna?
- What have you learned about "free expression" from Leon and Anna?

## RELATED BOOKS CHALLENGED FOR SIMILAR REASONS

Blume, Judy. **Then Again, Maybe I Won't.** *New York: Atheneum/Richard Jackson Books, 1982.*

This book has reported challenges for "sexual content" from 1980 to 1990. It was challenged at Port Neches Elementary School in Texas in 2010 for "sexual content or nudity."

Hentoff, Nat. **The Day They Came to Arrest the Book.** *New York: Delacorte Books for Young Readers, an imprint of Penguin Random House, 1982.*

In 1990 this book was challenged in Albemarle County schools in Charlottesville, Virginia, because it offers an inflammatory challenge to authoritarian roles.

Jukes, Mavis. **The Guy Book: An Owner's Manual.** *New York: Crown Books, an imprint of Random House, 2002.*

In 2002 this book was challenged, but retained at the Lockwood (Montana) Middle School library by parents who objected to what they believe to be misleading, sexually explicit material.

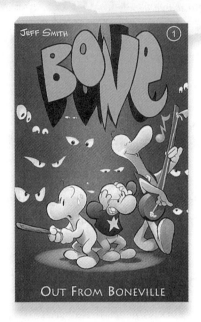

*Jeff Smith*

# Bone series

*New York: Graphix, an imprint of Scholastic, 2005–2009*

**OUT FROM BONEVILLE** (2005), **THE FIRST** novel in the series, introduces the Bone cousins, Phoney, Smiley, and Fone, as they are chased out of town because Phoney tries one of his notorious scams. The three become separated and aren't reunited until after they have outrun the rat creatures and crossed the mysterious Valley. They eventually find one another at Barrelhaven Tavern where they meet Thorn and her mysterious grandmother, Gran'ma Ben. It's not long before they realize that The Valley is in trouble, and they must help rid the area of the evil Lord of the Locusts. The eight books that follow span a year in the life of the Bone cousins as they weave in and out of the lives of humans and animals in The Valley. Fone falls for Thorn, Phoney continues his old habits of plotting outlandish scams, and Smiley simply follows along. There are a host of other characters—some good, and some evil: Lucius Down, the tavern owner; Kingdork, the leader of the rat creatures; the fearless Red Dragon, who has a past relationship with Gran'ma Ben; Ted, a very small insect that's a friend of the Red Dragon; The Hooded One, slave of the Lord of the Locusts; Rock Jaw, a large mountain lion. In *Crown of Horns,* the last book in the series, Thorn, Gran'ma Ben, and the Bone cousins are engaged in one last attempt to defend The Valley and prevent the return of the Lord of the Locusts. Filled with action and adventure, the theme of good vs. evil is brought to a dramatic conclusion.

The *Bone* series began as a black-and-white comic strip and grew into a series of epic comic books that Jeff Smith published himself. The adventures were later purchased by Graphix/Scholastic and published as graphic novels. Color was applied, the reviewing media took notice, and libraries began purchasing them. *Booklist* (October 15, 2004) reviews *The Complete Cartoon Epic in One Volume* (2004) and states, "The compilation makes it evident how fully formed Smith's vision was from the very beginning."

*The Horn Book Guide* (April 1, 2006) calls *The Great Cow Race* "inventive." *Booklist* reviewed an earlier printing of the book (July 1, 1996) and says, "Fantasy doesn't come at the expense of the humor and charm."

*School Library Journal* (January 1, 2007) doesn't find *Dragonslayer* as exciting as the first three books, but the reviewer does recognize that "what the story lacks in plot, it makes up for in character development." The reviewer for *Library Journal* (May 1, 2003) praises *Treasure Hunters,* #8 in the series, for its "adventure, comedy, and imagination." *Booklist* (September 1, 2004) recommends the books for ages 9–12, and notes that Jeff Smith has an "uncommon capability for switching gears from drama to humor." *Voice of Youth Advocates* (February 1, 2005) comments on the "detailed images and character relationships." *Publishers Weekly* (January 19, 2009) reviews *Crown of Horns,* the last book in the series, and says, "Smith expertly combines all the best elements of fantasy epics."

## The Books

(The publication year stated is for the full-color editions)

> *Out from Boneville,* 2005
> *The Great Cow Race,* 2005
> *Eyes of the Storm,* 2006
> *The Dragonslayer,* 2006
> *Rock Jaw: Master of the Eastern Border,* 2007
> *Old Man's Cave,* 2007
> *Ghost Circles,* 2008
> *Treasure Hunters,* 2008
> *Crown of Horns,* 2009

## CHALLENGES

According to data collected by the ALA's Office for Intellectual Freedom, the entire *Bone* series was #10 on the Top Ten Most Frequently Challenged Books List in 2013 because of "political viewpoint, racism, and violence."

A New Jersey parent challenged the entire series in 2009 because she felt it unsuited for the elementary school students. The institution involved asked to remain anonymous, and the status of the challenge is unknown. In 2010 a parent in Apple Valley, Minnesota, challenged the series at her son's elementary school because of "sexual situations between characters." In 2011 a parent lodged a challenge against book #4, *Dragonslayer,* in a New Mexico elementary school because of "illustrations that depict smoking and drinking." The parent bypassed procedure and took the book to a school board member who then took it to the principal. The principal removed the entire series from the school library. In the same year, the entire *Bone* series was challenged at Crestview Elementary School in Graham, Texas. The series was placed on a restricted shelf because it was considered "not appropriate for age group."

According to the 2012–2013 Texas ACLU Report on Banned and Challenged Books, the entire series was challenged, but retained at the Colleyville Elementary School in the Grapeville-Colleyville Independent School District because of "violence or horror." During the same school year, *The Great Cow Race* was challenged, but retained at the Whitley Road Elementary School in the Keller Independent School District. The reasons cited: "politically, racially, or socially offensive."

## AWARDS AND ACCOLADES

ALA/ALSC Graphic Novel List Update 2013
*Bone: Out from Boneville,* grades 6–8

ALA/ALSC Best of the Best Graphic Novels
*Bone: Out from Boneville,* grades 3–5

### Eisner Awards (for Artistic Excellence in the Comic Book Industry)

Jeff Smith has won in the following categories:

2005  Best Graphic Album Reprint: *Bone One-Volume Edition*
1998  Best Humor Writer/Artist: Humor: Jeff Smith
1995  Best Continuing Series
1995  Best Humor Writer Publication
1995  Best Writer/Artist: Humor: Jeff Smith
1994  Best Humor Publication
1994  Best Serialized Story: *The Great Cow Race*

1994  Best Continuing Series
1994  Best Writer/Artist
1993  Best Humor Publication

**Harvey Awards** (for Achievement in Comic Books)

Jeff Smith has won in the following categories:

2005  Best Cartoonist (Writer/Artist)
2005  Best Graphic Album of Previously Published Work:
      *Bone: One-Volume Edition*
2003  Best Cartoonist (Writer/Artist)
2000  Best Cartoonist (Writer/Artist)
1999  Body of Work in 1998, including *Bone* series
1997  Best Cartoonist (Writer/Artist)
1996  Best Cartoonist (Writer/Artist)
1995  Best Cartoonist (Writer/Artist)
1994  Best Cartoonist (Writer/Artist)
1994  Special Award for Humor
1994  Best Graphic Album of Previously Published Work:
      *The Complete Bone Adventures*; reissued in color as
      *Bone: Out from Boneville*

**OFFICIAL PUBLISHER'S WEBSITE**

www.boneville.com
www.scholastic.com/bone/books.htm

**FURTHER READING**

**The Author/Illustrator**

www.scholastic.com/teachers/contributor/jeff-smith-0
Chipman, Ian. "Talking with Jeff Smith." *Booklist* 108 (March 15, 2012): 36.
Fine, Jana. "The Heart, Soul, and Brain of Boneville: An Interview with Jeff Smith." *Young Adult Library Services* 1 (Fall 2002): 38–40.
"Jeff Smith." *Contemporary Authors* online, 2011. Books and Authors. Gale.

MacDonald, Heidi. "Jeff Smith on 'Bone.'" *Publishers Weekly* 25 (October 18, *2004): 34.*

## The Books

Filipi, David. *Jeff Smith: Bone and Beyond.* Illus. by Jeff Smith. Columbus: Ohio State University, Wexner Center for the Arts, 2008. 96 p.

Smith, Jeff. "Graphic Novels—Why in the World Do I Do It?" *Booklist* 102 (March 15, 2006): 64.

www.scholastic.com/teachers/lesson-plan/using-graphic-novels-children -and-teens-guide-teachers-and-librarians#top.

## Censorship

www.ala.org/offices/oif/ifissues/graphicnovels.

http://cbldf.org/banned-comic/banned-challenged-comics/case-study -bone. Comic Book Legal Defense Fund, 2010.

## For Listening and Viewing

www.youtube.com/watch?v = RDtetkEnYMA. Wexner Center for the Arts, May 11, 2009. In this video, fans of Jeff Smith talk about his impact on the field of comic books and graphic novels.

www.youtube.com/watch?v = QzJBAWec5uE. Comics on Comics, June 16, 2008. Jeff Smith talks about his favorite comic over time and discusses the *Bone* series.

## TALKING WITH READERS ABOUT THE ISSUES

- What is so appealing about the *Bone* series? Is it the adventure, the humor, or the elements of fantasy?
- The series has been challenged in elementary schools because some feel that it is "unsuited for age group." How do you answer this charge? Who is the audience for the books?
- There are others who are offended by the series because of the "sexual relationships." What relationship in the series is the center of this complaint? How are the adventures and quests about much more than one relationship?
- Others have challenged the books because they find them "socially offensive." Analyze the characters and the plots to determine what

is meant by "socially offensive." Had you noticed these things before you were asked to point them out?

- Role-play a scene where you defend the "literary merits" of the series to a parent or teacher.

## RELATED BOOKS CHALLENGED FOR SIMILAR REASONS

*Santat, Dan.* **Sidekicks.** *New York: Arthur A. Levine Books, an imprint of Scholastic, 2011. 224 p.*

According to the 2011–2012 Texas ACLU Report of Banned and Challenged Books, this volume was banned from Helen Park Elementary School in the Nederland Independent School District because of "profanity."

*Straczynski, J. Michael, John Romita, Jr., and Scott Hanna.* **Amazing Spider-Man: Revelations Vol. 2.** *New York: Marvel Comics, 2002.*

In 2009, a mother challenged this comic book at the Norris Elementary School in Millard, Nebraska, because of the "sexual undertones" and "lack of literary value." Marvel Comics recommends the book for ages 12–up. The status of the challenge is unknown.

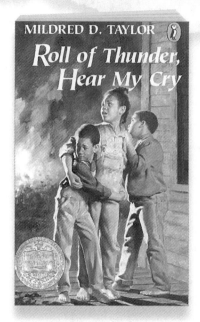

*Mildred D. Taylor*

# Roll of Thunder, Hear My Cry

*New York: Dial, 1976*

SET IN RURAL MISSISSIPPI DURING THE Great Depression, nine-year-old Cassie Logan tells the story of her family's struggle against poverty and their determination to keep its most cherished possession—four hundred acres of farmland. The cotton crop doesn't provide enough income to maintain the land and feed the three generations of Logans who live under one roof. Harlan Granger, the white man whose family owned the land before Grandpa Logan purchased it in 1887, is determined to get the land back and restore the original Granger plantation. Both of Cassie's parents work to earn enough money to pay the farm debt. Her dad is away laying track for the railroad, and her mother teaches at the black school. Big Ma, Cassie's grandmother, sells milk and eggs in the nearby town of Strawberry.

To add to the family problems, the Logans are victims of racism. In Mr. Barnett's store, they are forced to wait until the white customers have been helped. Cassie also tangles with Lillian Jean Simms, a white girl, on the sidewalk outside the store. Then, as the Logan children take their long walk on the dirt road to school, they are splattered with mud by the school bus that takes the white children to their school. Things get worse with the threat of the Night Riders, and Mary Logan is fired from her teaching position for lodging a protest against the secondhand textbooks that the black students are forced to use. Sharecroppers are burned out, a black boy is accused of murder, and the town organizes a lynching party to go after the kid.

The reviewer for *Kirkus* (October 1, 1976) notes that the "characters are drawn with quiet affection." Betsy Hearne in her *Booklist* (October

1, 1976) starred review says the "novel shows the rich inner rewards of black pride, love, and independence." Sally Holmes Holtze, reviewer for *Horn Book Magazine* (December 1976), says the "characters are so carefully drawn that one might assume the book to be autobiographical." Upon the publication of this Newbery Medal book, Emily R. Moore, a contributor to the *Interracial Books for Children Bulletin*, made a prediction that it would become a classic.

Other books in the Logan family saga: *Song of Trees* (1962); *Let the Circle Be Unbroken* (1974); *The Road to Memphis* (1983); *The Friendship* (1985); *The Well* (1990); and *The Land* (2000).

### CHALLENGES

According to the ALA's Office for Intellectual Freedom, this Newbery Medal book ranked #66 on the Top 100 Banned/Challenged Books List: 2000–2009. It was #9 on the Ten Most Frequently Challenged Books List of 2002.

In 1993 the novel was removed from the ninth-grade reading list at the Arcadia High School in Louisiana because of "racial bias." The novel was challenged in 1998 in O'Hara Park Middle School classrooms in Oakley, California, because it uses racial epithets. In 2000 the novel was challenged in Chapman Elementary School libraries in Huntsville, Alabama, because the book uses racial slurs in dialogue to make points about racism.

In 2004 the novel was challenged, but retained as a part of the Seminole County school curriculum in Florida despite the concerns of an African American couple that found the book inappropriate for their thirteen-year-old son. The award-winning book depicts the life of an African American family in rural Mississippi in the 1930s and uses the word "nigger." According to the *Orlando Sentinel*, Debra Drake, the parent, said, "A middle-school class is an inappropriate place to discuss racial issues because the students are too young to understand the material." The book was challenged, but retained at Arthur Intermediate School in Kennedale (Texas) Independent School District in 2006 because of "racism."

## AWARDS AND ACCOLADES

2003 Mildred D. Taylor named NSK Neustadt Laureate by *World Literature Today*

1997 Alan Award

1979 Young Reader's Choice Award: Junior (Pacific Northwest)

1976 *The Horn Book* Fanfare Honor List

1977 John Newbery Medal

1977 American Library Association Notable Books for Children

1977 National Book Award Finalist

1977 *Boston Globe-Horn Book* Honor Book

1970–1982 *Booklist* Best of the Best Books

1970–1980 *New York Times* Book Review Best Children's Books

## FURTHER READING

### The Author

Crowe, Chris. *Presenting Mildred D. Taylor.* New York: Cengage Gale, 1999. (Twayne's United States Authors Series).

Fogelman, Phyllis J. "Mildred D. Taylor." *Horn Book Magazine* 53, no. 4 (August, 1977): 410–14.

"Mildred D. Taylor." *Contemporary Authors* online, 2005. Books and Authors. Gale.

Taylor, Mildred D. "Growing Up with Stories." *Booklist* 87 (December 1, 1990): 700–741.

### The Book

Harper, Mary Turner. "Merger and Metamorphosis in the Fiction of Mildred D. Taylor." *Children's Literature Quarterly* 13 (1988): 75–80.

Rees, David. "The Color of Skin: Mildred Taylor." In *The Marble in the Water,* 104–13. Boston: Horn Book, 1980.

Scales, Pat R. "Book Strategies: *Roll of Thunder, Hear My Cry* by Mildred Taylor." *Book Links* (January, 1995): 12–14.

Smith, Karen Patricia. "A Chronicle of Family Honor: Balancing Rage and Triumph in the Novels of Mildred D. Taylor." In *African American Voices in Young Adult Literature,* 247–76. Lanham, MD: Scarecrow, 1994.

Taylor, Mildred D. "Newbery Award Acceptance Speech." *Horn Book Magazine.* 53, no. 4 (August, 1977): 401–9.

**Censorship**

Bertin, Joan, executive director of the National Coalition Against Censorship. "Letter from NCAC to Protest the Challenging of *Roll of Thunder, Hear My Cry.*" January 26, 2004. www.ncac.org/education/related/20040126~FL-Seminole_County~NCAC_Letter_to_Seminole_County_School_Board.cfm.

Wollman-Bonilla, Julie E. "Outrageous Viewpoints: Teachers' Criteria for Rejecting Works of Children's Literature." *Language Arts* 75, no. 4 (April 1998): 287–95.

**For Listening and Viewing**

www.moviesplanet.com/movies/25045/roll-of-thunder-hear-my-cry. Movie Planet, 1978. This is the full movie of *Roll of Thunder, Hear My Cry.*

## TALKING WITH READERS ABOUT THE ISSUES

- Talk about the difference between overt and covert racism. Cite evidence from the novel that the Logan family experiences both types of racism.
- The school bus driver makes the white children laugh when he splatters mud on the black children as they walk to school. What do the Logan children do to get back at the white bus driver?
- Why do the other teachers at the black school consider Mary Logan a "disruptive maverick"?
- How does the racial discrimination in the novel reflect the time and place of the story?
- How might the novel be used to help readers understand rather than deny that racial discrimination exists?

## RELATED BOOKS CHALLENGED FOR SIMILAR REASONS

Armstrong, William H. **Sounder.** *Illustrated by James Barkley. New York: HarperCollins, 1969.*

Challenged, but retained in the Rockingham, New York County schools for use of the word "nigger" and because the main character, a black share-cropper, is called "boy."

Gaines, Ernest J. **The Autobiography of Miss Jane Pittman.** *New York: Bantam, 1971.*

Challenged in 2006 as an eighth-grade district-wide reading assignment in the Puyallup, Washington, schools because "racial slurs and stereotyping are used throughout the book, as well as scenes of sex, rape, and implied incest." The school board voted to uphold an earlier decision by a district committee requiring eighth-graders to read the novel. In 1995 the novel was pulled from a seventh-grade class in Conroe, Texas, after complaints about racial slurs. School officials later reinstated it.

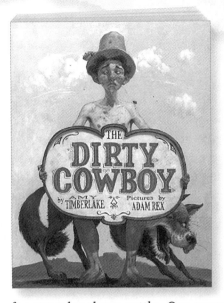

*Amy Timberlake*

# The Dirty Cowboy

*Illustrated by Adam Rex. New York: Farrar, Straus & Giroux, 2003*

THE COWBOY LIVES ON THE NEW MEX-ico range where he spends his days with his horse and his dog looking for stray longhorn cattle. One morning the cowboy decides that it must be time for a bath because fleas were attacking him. He even discovered tumbleweeds in his clothes. He grabs a bar of lye soap, mounts his horse, and calls for "Dawg" to follow him to the river. When they reach their destination, the cowboy tells "Dawg," "No one touches these clothes but me. Hear?" "Dawg" does as he is told, and when the cowboy emerges from the river with a fresh smell, he's got a problem greater than a few fleas. The cowboy is so clean, and smells so good that "Dawg" doesn't recognize him. This is where the real problem begins. "Dawg," whose real name is Eustace Shackelford Montana, won't let the cowboy near the clothes. They tussle and wrestle until everything but the cowboy's boots and hat are in shreds. After the fight, cowboy is about as dirty as he was before taking a bath, and when "Dawg" smells "tumbleweed, prickly pear, and wet mud," he finally recognizes his cowboy. As the sun is setting on the range, the cowboy walks home "naked as a nickel" with Eustace and his horse by his side. The illustrations, painted in earth tones to covey the New Mexico desert setting, are humorous and filled with action. Adam Rex cleverly conceals the cowboy's private parts—in one illustration when he stands up in the river, there is a frog sitting on a rock in front of him. In the final illustration, the cowboy, his horse, and, of course, "Dawg" are shadows against the light of the moon and stars.

Todd Morning, reviewer for *Booklist* (September 1, 2003), says the book is "a simple, slapstick tale that is sure to elicit some giggles." He recommends the book for K–Gr. 2. *School Library Journal* (September 1, 2003) recommends the books for k–Gr. 4 and calls it "a fun look at life on the range." *Publishers Weekly* (July 14, 2003) states, "Transcending the cowboy-tale genre, this raucous romp should tickle bath-averse children everywhere." The starred review recommends it for ages 4–8. The reviewer for *Kirkus* (June 15, 2003) gave the book a star and states that the illustrator keeps the "Legion of Decency off his case in numerous artful ways." Aaron Latham, reviewer for the *New York Times Book Review* (December 2003), says of the nameless cowboy, "He is a cowboy even when taking a bath."

❝ Censorship of a kid's book is nothing short of denying other parents their rights."

—Adam Rex, illustrator of The Dirty Cowboy

## CHALLENGES

According to the Texas ACLU Annual Report 2005–2006, the picture book was removed from the library at the W. C. Andrews Primary School in Portland, Texas, because the "principal didn't want the book in the library." The Texas ACLU reported a challenge in 2009 at the Kinkeade Early Childhood School in Irving because of "sexual content or nudity." The book was retained.

In 2012 in Annville, Pennsylvania, a couple objected to the book's "depiction of a nude cowboy whose private parts are covered by various objects in the book's illustrations." According to the *Harrisburg Patriot,* the Annville-Cleona School Board voted 8–0 to remove the book from the district libraries.

## AWARDS AND ACCOLADES

2004   Golden Kite Award for Picture Book Text
2004   First Prize in the Marion Vannett Ridgway Awards
2004   International Reading Association Notable Book
Parents Choice Gold Medal
*Bulletin of Center for Children's Books* Blue Ribbon

## AUTHOR AND ILLUSTRATOR'S OFFICIAL WEBSITE

http://amytimberlake.com

www.adamrex.com

## FURTHER READING

### The Author

www.childrensliteraturenetwork.org/aifolder/aipages/ai_t/tmbrlake.html.

"Amy Timberlake." *Chicago Tribune A&E,* August 1, 2013. http://articles
.chicagotribune.com/2013–08–01/entertainment/ct-prj-meet-lit
-fest-authors-timberlake-20130801_1_library-card-music-library
-checkout-desk.

"Amy Timberlake." *Contemporary Authors* online, 2007. Books and Authors.
Gale.

### The Illustrator

Herreras, Mari. "Adam Rex Gets a Big Head (. . . Not Really). *Tucson
Weekly* (Arizona), March 7, 2013. www.tucsonweekly.com/tucson/
adam-rex-gets-a-big-head-not-really/Content?oid=3658112.

### The Book

Timberlake, Amy. "Help! The Writing Process of *The Dirty Cowboy*: From
Family Story to Published Books," 2005. www.underdown.org/
writing_the_dc.htm.

### Censorship

Baldassarro, R. Wolf. "Banned Books Awareness: *The Dirty Cowboy.*"
Posted April 3, 2012. http://bannedbooks.world.edu/2012/04/23/
banned-books-awareness-the-dirty-cowboy.

Brad Rhen. "*The Dirty Cowboy* Author Book Ban 'Ridiculous.'" *Lebanon
Daily News* (Pennsylvania), April 20, 2012. www.ldnews.com/
ci_20443324/dirty-cowboy-author-book-ban-ridiculous.

Finan, Christopher. "Freedom to Read: Book Banning Is No Laughing
Matter." *Durango Herald* (Colorado), September 29, 2012. www
.durangoherald.com/article/20120929/OPINION02/120929484.

http://ncacblog.wordpress.com/2012/05/16/the-so-not-dirty-cowboy
    -author-speaks.

White, Tim. "'The Dirty Cowboy' is about a Lot More Than One Book,"
    *Patriot-News* (Pennsylvania), June 9, 2012. www.pennlive.com/
    editorials/index.ssf/2012/06/the_dirty_cowboy_mess.html.

**For Listening and Viewing**

www.youtube.com/watch?v=v805W9tzRhw. March 25, 2010. Amy
    Timberlake talks about *The Dirty Cowboy*.

## TALKING WITH READERS ABOUT THE ISSUES

- Why does this book make you laugh? Is it the story, or the pictures? Or is it the fact that the cowboy is naked?
- How dirty is the cowboy? How long do you think it has been since he had a bath?
- Discuss why "Dawg" won't let cowboy near his clothes. How is "Dawg" doing what cowboy told him to do?
- Explain how cowboy tries to convince "Dawg" that he really is his cowboy.
- There are people who don't like this book because the cowboy is naked. Let's look at the illustrations. How are the cowboy's private parts cleverly hidden?
- Discuss whether the book would be a good story if the cowboy took a bath in his clothes. How realistic would that be?

## RELATED BOOKS CHALLENGED FOR SIMILAR REASONS

Carle, Eric. **Draw Me a Star**. *Philomel, an imprint of Penguin Random House, 1992.*

According to the Texas ACLU 2001–2002 Annual Report, this book was challenged, but retained at Harmony Elementary School in San Antonio for "sexual content." The parent objected to the nude tissue paper forms of a man and a woman. The book was restricted at Weatherford Elementary in Plano because "several parents felt the illustration of the man and woman was inappropriate for kindergarten or even 3rd–5th grade. Too early to introduce private parts outside of guided health instruction."

*Kuskin, Karla.* **The Philharmonic Gets Dressed.** *Illus. by Marc Simont. New York: HarperCollins, 1986.*

According to the Texas ACLU Report of Banned and Challenged Books: 2002–2003, this book was challenged at the R. Q. Sims Intermediate School in the Mexia Independent School District because of "sexual content." The book shows members of the orchestra getting dressed for a performance, including illustrations of them bathing, powdering, shaving, and dressing.

*Sendak, Maurice.* **In the Night Kitchen.** *New York: Harper and Row (now HarperCollins), 1970.*

This book was #24 on the American Library Association's 100 Most Banned/ Challenged Books List 2000–2009. The earliest recorded challenge was in 1977 when it was removed from the Norridge School library in Illinois due to "nudity for no purpose." The same year, in Springfield, Missouri, someone expurgated the book by drawing shorts on Mickey. In 2006, parents getting help from Called2Action challenged the book in Wake County schools in North Carolina. This group is a Christian group that says its mission is to "promote and defend our shared family and social values."

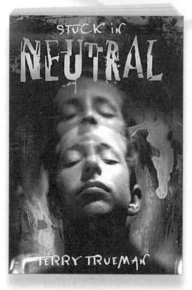

*Terry Trueman*

# Stuck in Neutral

*New York: HarperCollins, 2001*

**FOURTEEN-YEAR-OLD SHAWN MCDANIEL** has cerebral palsy and is locked inside his head, unable to focus his eyes or communicate at all. He does have thoughts about a lot of things, and he relates them as he narrates his story. According to Shawn, and unknown to those around him, he has a "special ability" to recall every conversation that he has heard, and all events in his life. He enjoys eavesdropping on his older brother and sister and their friends, and he credits them with his education about matters of life. He observes their interaction and he wonders: "What does your arm feel like throwing a baseball? What do your lips feel when you kiss somebody?"

Shawn's parents have been divorced for ten years, and he realizes that he is the cause. His father, a journalist and Pulitzer Prize–winning poet, simply couldn't deal with his son's condition. Though his father visits the family, Shawn has counted the number of times that he and his father have been alone together: "six times in fourteen years." During one visit, Shawn's father says, "Maybe I should just end your pain." This is when Shawn becomes convinced that his father is planning to kill him. Yet he doesn't doubt that his father loves him. The reader is left to wonder if Shawn's father follows through with his plan.

Reviewers have praised the book for its unusual point of view and tone. *Publisher's Weekly* (July 11, 2000) states, "The strength of the novel lies in the father-son dynamic." *School Library Journal* (July 1, 2000) calls the book an "intriguing premise," and states that it will challenge readers to "look beyond people's surfaces." They recommend it for grades 5–9. *Voice of Youth Advocates* (December 1, 2000) says, "Trueman explores the what-ifs, creating a compelling teenage character with a strong affirming personality." The *Kirkus* (June 30, 2000) reviewer writes, "Shawn will stay with readers, not for what he does, but for what he is and has made of himself." Finally, Ilene Cooper states in *Booklist* (July 27, 2000), "Readers spend the entire book inside Shawn's head, a place so vivid, so unique they will be hard pressed to forget its mix of heaven and hell." She recommends the novel for grades 6–10.

*Life Happens Next* (2012) is the sequel to *Stuck in Neutral* and answers the questions raised by those troubled by the open ending of Trueman's first novel. In this novel, Shawn has celebrated his fifteenth birthday and his mom takes in her orphaned Down syndrome cousin. Debi and Shawn have a special connection, and it's through Debi that Shawn comes to realize, "I'm more alive than I've ever been before." In the "Author's Note," Trueman writes, "My stories are an attempt to expand my readers' and my own compassion, empathy, and understanding of the lives of people struggling and dealing with extraordinary challenges and situations. I hope this sequel to *Stuck in Neutral* achieves that higher purpose."

> " I cannot say it pleases me that *Stuck in Neutral* is on various banned book lists. Every reader robbed of being changed for the better by reading this novel is being harmed."
>
> —Terry Trueman, author of *Stuck in Neutral*

## CHALLENGES

The 2002–2003 Report of the Texas ACLU lists a challenge at Franklin Middle School in Abilene, Texas, for "profanity/language and sexual content." The book was retained. The book was also challenged at Crawford Middle School in Crawford, Texas, for "profanity or inappropriate language, sexual content, violence or horror."

In 2003 the novel was challenged, but retained on the reading list for eighth-graders at the Evansville High School in Wisconsin despite concerns about profanity, sexual imagery, and violence.

A Creekwood Middle School parent in Humble, Texas, challenged the book in 2012 for "obscene" language and because he didn't feel the discussion of "euthanasia age-appropriate." The district pledged to "screen books closer." The school board also voted to take a closer look at guest speakers after they received a concern that Trueman used "foul language" when he visited Atascocita Middle School. The librarian called his visit to the school "pleasant and professional."

## AWARDS AND ACCOLADES

2005  Books Change Lives Award, California Center for the Book
2002  Kentucky Bluegrass Award
2001  Michael L. Printz Honor Book
2001  ALA Best Books for Young Adults
2001  ALA Quick Pick for Reluctant Young Adult Readers
2001  New York Public Library Best Read for Teens
2000  ALA *Booklist* Books for Youth Editor's Choice
2000  ALA *Booklist* Top 10 Youth First Novels
2000  *Parents Guide to Children's Media:* Outstanding Achievement in Fiction

## AUTHOR'S OFFICIAL WEBSITE

www.terrytrueman.com

## FURTHER READING

### The Author

Arth, Joan. "Author Profile: Terry Trueman." *Library Media Collection* 27, no. 1 (August/September 2008): 36–37.
Halls, Kelly Milner, "The Truth about Trueman: An Interview with Terry Trueman." *Voice of Youth Advocates* 25, no. 5 (December 2002): 346–47.
Squicciarini, Stephanie A. "The Worst Day Writing Is Better Than the Best Day at Work." *Public Libraries* 44, no. 4 (July/August 2005): 205–7.

### The Book

"The Power of Reading *Stuck in Neutral*." *Teen Librarian Toolbox*, August 9, 2012. www.teenlibrariantoolbox.com/2012/08/the-power-of -reading-stuck-in-neutral.html.

## Censorship

"Blogging Censorship: Talking 'Dark' YA Lit with Terry Trueman."
*National Coalition Against Censorship*, May 30, 2012. http://
ncacblog.wordpress.com/tag/stuck-in-neutral.

"Censorship Dateline." *Newsletter on Intellectual Freedom* 61 (July 2012):
153–84.

Janacek, Rick. "Changes Expected after Outcry over Book Selection." *The
Tribune* (Humble, Texas), May 14, 2012. http://ourtribune.com/
article.php?id=13614.

## For Listening and Viewing

www.youtube.com/watch?v=dS8PUsRjeQo. A student portrays Shawn
McDaniel, the main character in *Stuck in Neutral.*

www.youtube.com/watch?v=8nNKJnDnZrk. April 12, 2009. Terry
Trueman talks with Ed Spicer about *Stuck in Neutral* and his entire
body of work.

www.youtube.com/watch?v=uBrLtIlFvSQ; www.youtube.com/
watch?v=AzjhEZAE0dk. September 11, 2007. A teen patron at the
North Central Regional Library in Wenatchee, Washington, conducts
this two-part interview with Terry Trueman.

## TALKING WITH READERS ABOUT THE ISSUES

• How does Shawn's condition affect his entire family?
• Discuss how Cindy and Paul's friends react to Shawn. How is Shawn a victim of discrimination from those around him?
• Shawn is locked inside his own mind because he can't communicate. How are his thoughts and sexual fantasies similar to most adolescents?
• Shawn's father wins a Pulitzer Prize for a poem that he wrote about his son. Discuss whether his father's poem is an effort to come to terms with his son's condition.
• Shawn's father appears on TV talk shows. How might audiences think that he is exploiting his son?
• What is euthanasia? Why is Shawn so convinced that his father is trying to kill him?
• The novel has an open ending, leaving Shawn's fate to the reader. What do you think happens?

- Discuss how Shawn's story may cause readers to become more sensitive to people with disabilities.

## RELATED BOOKS CHALLENGED FOR SIMILAR REASONS

*Going, K. L.* **Fat Kid Rules the World.** *New York: Penguin, 2003.*

This 2004 Michael Printz honor book was removed from the Pickens, South Carolina, middle and high school library shelves in 2007 because "the language, the sexual references, and drug use are not appropriate for middle-school students." It was also challenged as a suggested summer reading at the Alsip Prairie Junior High School in Illinois because the book is "laced with profanity and other mature content."

*Wittlinger, Ellen.* **Hard Love.** *New York: Simon and Schuster, 1999.*

In 2009 this Printz Honor book (2000) was challenged in West Bend, Wisconsin, along with numerous children's and young adult titles because the "the books are obscene and the sexual content inappropriate for young readers."

# Resources for Teaching Young Readers about the First Amendment

## FICTION

Blume, Judy. Illus. by Jane Wattenberg. **Places I Never Meant to Be.** *New York: Simon Pulse, 2001*

This collection of twelve short stories, written by writers whose works have been banned or challenged, has a central theme: the main characters find themselves in places they never meant to be.

Brande, Robin. **Evolution, Me & Other Freaks of Nature.** *New York: Knopf, an imprint of Penguin Random House, 2009*

Mean Reese, a high school freshman, knows firsthand that it's lonely to stick up for one's rights, but when a favorite science teacher faces off with censors over a unit on evolution, she finds a few "open-minded" friends who are willing to join forces to stand by their teacher.

Bryant, Jen. **Ringside 1925: Views from the Scopes Trial.** *New York: Knopf, an imprint of Penguin Random House, 2008*

A series of poems, in the voices of real and fictional characters, tells the story of the famous Scopes Monkey Trial that took place in Dayton, Tennessee, in 1925, and caused a few young people to think about the First Amendment and academic freedom.

*Clements, Andrew. Illustrated by Brian Selznick and Salvatore Murdocca.* **The Landry News.** *New York: Simon and Schuster, 2000*
Clara is disappointed when she arrives at Denton Elementary School and is placed in the class of a burned-out fifth-grade teacher. She writes an editorial about him in her newspaper, *The Landry News.* Then the paper evolves into a class project and the students learn lessons about free speech and responsibility when the principal uses the paper as a reason to get rid of the teacher.

*Crutcher, Chris.* **The Sledding Hill.** *New York: HarperCollins, 2005*
Fourteen-year-old Eddie takes direction from the ghost of a deceased friend as he battles a conservative minister who is leading a censorship war at his school.

*Cushman, Karen.* **The Loud Silence of Francine Green.** *Electronic Book Text. Boston: Harcourt Houghton Mifflin, 2006*
Francine Green has always been taught to keep her ideas and beliefs to herself, but she suddenly finds her voice and the need to express it when outspoken and opinionated Sophie Bowman transfers into her class and challenges her to think about issues like free speech, the atom bomb, the existence of God, and the way people treat one another.

*Downey, Jen Swann.* **The Ninja Librarians.** *Naperville, Illinois: Source Books, an imprint of Casablanca Press, 2014*
Dorrie and her brother chase their dog into a closet in their local public library and discover the Ninja Librarians, a secret society formed to preserve the words of writers whose works have been censored through the ages. There is a cautionary message in this book of adventure, mystery, and fantasy.

*Facklam, Margery.* **The Trouble with Mothers.** *New York: Clarion, an imprint of Harcourt Houghton Mifflin, 1989*
Eighth-grader Luke Troy is devastated when his mother, a teacher, writes a historical novel that is considered pornography by some people in the community where they live.

*Hentoff, Nat.* **The Day They Came to Arrest the Book.** *New York: Dell, an imprint of Penguin Random House, 1985*
Students in a high school English class protest the study of *Huckleberry Finn* until the editor of the school newspaper uncovers other cases of censorship and in a public hearing reveals the truth behind the mysterious disappearance of certain library books and the resignation of the school librarian.

*Krensky, Stephen. Illustrated by Madeline Sorel.* **The Printer's Apprentice.**
*New York: Dell paperback, an imprint of Penguin Random House, 1995*
Set in New York City in 1735, Gus Croft is only ten years old when he delivers a message for John Peter Zenger, a printer who was arrested for criticizing the governor, to his defense lawyer, and in the process of the trial Gus begins to understand the freedom of the press.

*Lasky, Kathryn.* **Memoirs of a Bookbat.** *Boston: Harcourt Houghton Mifflin, 1994*
Fourteen-year-old Harper Jessup, an avid reader, runs away because she feels that her individual rights are threatened when her parents, born-again fundamentalists, lodge a public promotion of book censorship.

*Martin, Ann Matthews.* **Claudia and the First Thanksgiving.** *New York: Scholastic, 1995*
Claudia has written a play for third graders as a Thanksgiving celebration, but she finds herself in the middle of a censorship case when some parents take issue with her not-so-traditional presentation of the subject. (Baby Sitters Club, no. 91)

*Patron, Susan.* **Lucky for Good.** *New York: Atheneum Books for Young Readers, an imprint of Simon & Schuster, 2011*
The third book in a trilogy, eleven-year-old Lucky continues her interest in Charles Darwin and the theory of evolution, but issues arise when Miles's mother who has just gotten out of prison where she found religion challenges Lucky's beliefs, and forbids Miles to take part in such discussions.

*Peck, Richard.* **The Last Safe Place on Earth.** *New York: Delacorte, an imprint of Penguin Random House, 1995*
The Tobin family is satisfied that Walden Woods is a quiet, safe community to rear three children. Then seven-year-old Marnie begins having night-

mares after a babysitter tells her that Halloween is "evil," and Todd and Diana, sophomores in high school, witness an organized group's attempt to censor books in their school library.

*Reed, M. K. Illustrated by Jonathan David Hill.* **Americus.** *New York: Roaring Brook, an imprint of Macmillan, 2011*

Americus public library is under attack by a right-wing religious group and ninth-grader Neal Barton, who is by nature quiet and reserved, finds himself in uncharted territory when he is thrust into an all-out defense of his favorite fantasy series.

*Winerip, Michael.* **Adam Canfield, the Last Reporter.** *Boston: Candlewick, 2009*

The school board has shut down the Harris Elementary/Middle School newspaper, *The Slash,* because of their coverage of past stories on a crooked principal, suspicious state test scores, and a dirty school election. Adam Canfield, the famed editor of the newspaper, is determined to find a way to get the banned newspaper going again.

## NONFICTION

*Burns, Kate.* **Censorship.** *Farmington Hills, Michigan: Greenhaven, an imprint of Cengage Gale, 2006*

Essays by historians and scholars examine issues related to censorship, which include primary documents like speeches, court cases, newspaper articles, and some personal testimony that support the arguments about controversial topics from the past to the present. (The History of Issues Series)

*Burns, Kate.* **Fighters Against Censorship.** *Farmington Hills, Michigan: Lucent Books, an imprint of Cengage Gale, 2004*

Spanning ancient to modern days, seven people are featured in this volume: James Madison, Theodore Schroeder, Emma Goldman, Pete Seeger, Tommy Smothers, Larry Flynt, and Mitchell Kapor. (History Makers, collective biography series)

*Conway, John Richard.* **A Look at the First Amendment: Freedom of Speech and Religion.** *Berkeley Heights, New Jersey: Enslow, 2009*
In clear and concise language, the author chronicles First Amendment cases, beginning with the 1735 court case that established freedom of the press and continuing with discussion of more recent issues related to the separation of church and state.

*Day, Nancy.* **Censorship, or Freedom of Expression?** *Minneapolis: Lerner, 2005*
Peppered with anecdotal accounts of how people respond to censorship, there is an examination of current issues related to movies, books, art, newspapers, the Internet, and government infringement on individual rights. (Pro/Con Series)

*Egendorf, Laura K., ed.* **Censorship.** *Farmington Hills, Michigan: Greenhaven, an imprint of Cengage Gale, 2002.*
Illustrated with political cartoons, this collection of articles by various people of authority discusses freedom of speech in our democracy; censorship issues in schools; whether or not pornography should be censored; and, whether the government should regulate art and pop art. (Examining Issues Through Political Cartoons Series)

*Feinman, Myke.* **The Crystal Skull Files: A First Amendment Fable for All Ages.** *Streator, Illinois: Ink and Feathers Comics, 1998*
There is comedy, suspense, and lessons to be learned in this continuation of the *Freedom Mystiques* series. Art is done in Bigfoot Popeye style.

*Gottfried, Ted.* **Censorship.** *Tarrytown, New York: Benchmark Books, 2005*
Case studies explain current and often-volatile issues related to the Internet, book censorship, hate speech, and motion picture ratings. A center section called "You Be the Judge" asks readers to debate specific real-life scenarios. (Open for Debate Series)

*Krensky, Stephen.* **The Bill of Rights.** *London: Marshall Cavendish, 2011*
The history of the Bill of Rights, how it came to be, why it is important, and how it applies to present-day issues that affect students. (The Documents of America Series)

*Krull, Kathleen. Illustrated by Anna DiVito.* **A Kid's Guide to America's Bill of Rights: Curfews, Censorship, and the 100-Pound Giant.** *New York: HarperCollins, 1999*
Anecdotes, case studies, humorous illustrations, and sidebars mask the history lesson of this kid-friendly discussion of the first ten amendments of the U.S. Constitution. Scenarios are presented that make these amendments applicable to daily life.

*Sherrow, Victoria.* **Censorship in Schools.** *Berkeley Heights, New Jersey: Enslow, 1996*
This documented text clearly defines censorship and traces the development of censorship in schools throughout history. A detailed discussion of problems of free expression in schools today includes censorship of literature, textbooks, student newspapers, and so on.

*Taylor-Butler, Christine.* **The Bill of Rights.** *New York: Scholastic Library Publishing, 2007*
Easy-to-read text and heavily illustrated for young readers, a very condensed history of the Bill of Rights leads to information about how these amendments apply to current issues. Sidebars, glossary, index augment the text. (A True Book Series)

# Bibliography: Professional Resources about Book Censorship and the Freedom to Read

Abel, Richard L. **Speaking Respect, Respecting Speech.** *1998. University of Chicago Press.*

Adams, Thelma, ed. **Censorship and First Amendment Rights: A Primer.** *1992. American Booksellers Foundation for Free Expression.*

Bald, Margaret. **Literature Suppressed on Religious Grounds.** *2011. Facts on File.*

Brown, Jean E. **Preserving Intellectual Freedom: Fighting Censorship in Our Schools.** *1995. National Council of Teachers of English.*

Coetzee, J. M. **Giving Offense: On Censorship.** *1997. University of Chicago Press.*

Foerstel, Herbert N. **Banned in the U.S.A.: A Reference Guide to Book Censorship in Schools and Public Libraries.** *1994. Greenwood.*

Green, Jonathan, and Nicholas J. Karolides. **The Encyclopedia of Censorship.** *2005. Facts on File.*

Hull, Mary. **Censorship in America: A Reference Handbook.** *1999. ABC-Clio.*

Johnson, Claudia. **Stifled Laughter: One Woman's Fight against Censorship.** *1994. Fulcrum.*

*Karolides, Nicholas J.* **Literature Suppressed on Political Grounds.** *2011. Facts on File.*

*Karolides, Nicholas J. and others.* **Censored Books: Critical Viewpoints.** *2001. Scarecrow.*

*Kennedy, Sheila Suess, ed.* **Free Expression in America: A Documentary History,** *1999. Greenwood.*

*Knuth, Rebecca.* **Burning Books and Leveling Libraries: Extremist Violence and Cultural Destruction.** *2006. Greenwood.*

*Lehr, Susan, ed.* **Battling Dragons: Issues and Controversy in Children's Literature.** *1995. Heinemann.*

*Lusted, Marcia Amidon.* **Banned Books.** *2013. ABDO.*

*Noble, William.* **Bookbanning in America: Who Bans Books?—and Why?** *1990. Paul S. Eriksson.*

*Reichman, Henry.* **Censorship and Selection: Issues and Answers for Schools.** *2001. American Library Association.*

*Sova, Dawn B.* **Literature Suppressed on Sexual Grounds.** *2011. Facts on File.*

*Sova, Dawn B.* **Literature Suppressed on Social Grounds.** *2011. Facts on File.*

*West, Mark.* **Trust Your Children: Voices against Censorship in Children's Literature.** *1997. Neal Schuman.*

# Rankings of Children's and Young Adult Books in the Top 100 Most Banned or Challenged Books List: 2000—2009

(# refers to the ranking on the list)

#1    *Harry Potter* (series) by J. K. Rowling
      "witchcraft"

#2    *Alice* (series) by Phyllis Reynolds Naylor
      "sexual references"

#3    *The Chocolate War* by Robert Cormier
      "sexual content, offensive language, & religious viewpoint"

#4    *And Tango Makes Three* by Justin Richardson/Peter Parnell
      "promotes homosexuality"

#7    *Scary Stories* (series) by Alvin Schwartz
      "too frightening, occult & Satanism"

#8    *His Dark Materials* (series) by Philip Pulman
      "anti-Christian message"

#11   *Fallen Angels* by Walter Dean Myers
      "profanity, racial epithets, & torture"

#12   *It's Perfectly Normal* by Robie H. Harris
      "sexual content"

#13    *Captain Underpants* (series) by Dav Pilkey
       "unruly behavior & offensive language"

#20    *King and King* by Linda de Haan
       "gay themes"

#23    *The Giver* by Lois Lowry
       "violent & sexual passages"

#24    *In the Night Kitchen* by Maurice Sendak
       "nudity"

#25    *Killing Mr. Griffin* by Lois Duncan
       "violence & language"

#27    *My Brother Sam Is Dead* by James Lincoln Collier
       "profanity & graphic violence"

#28    *Bridge to Terabithia* by Katherine Paterson
       "offensive language, witchcraft, & violence"

#29    *The Face on the Milk Carton* by Caroline B. Cooney
       "sexual content & undermines authority"

#37    *It's So Amazing* by Robie Harris
       "sexual content"

#42    *The Fighting Ground* by Avi
       "profanity"

#43    *Blubber* by Judy Blume
       "offensive language & cruelty to classmate"

#45    *Crazy Lady* by Jane Leslie Conly
       "objectionable language"

#52    *The Great Gilly Hopkins* by Katherine Paterson
       "explicit language"

#55    *Summer of My German Soldier* by Bette Greene
       "offensive racial stereotypes"

#59    *Olive's Ocean* by Kevin Henkes
       "sexual content & profanity"

#62    *The Stupids* (series) by Harry Allard
        "undermines authority"

#64    *Mick Harte Was Here* by Barbara Park
        "themes & language inappropriate for elementary school"

#66    *Roll of Thunder, Hear My Cry* by Mildred Taylor
        "racial bias"

#70    *Harris and Me* by Gary Paulsen
        "cultural insensitivity & offensive language"

#71    *Junie B. Jones* (series) by Barbara Park
        "poor social values"

#75    *Anastasia* (series) by Lois Lowry
        "profanity"

#79    *The Upstairs Room* by Johanna Reiss
        "profanity"

#84    *So Far from the Bamboo Grove* by Yoko Watkins
        "violence against women"

#87    *Tiger Eyes* by Judy Blume
        "alcohol, profanity, & sexual content"

#90    *A Wrinkle in Time* by Madeline L'Engle
        "promotes witchcraft & undermines religious beliefs"

#91    *Julie of the Wolves* by Jean Craighead George
        "profanity & sexual content"

#92    *The Boy Who Lost His Face* by Louis Sachar
        "profanity & obscene gestures"

#93    *Bumps in the Night* by Harry Allard
        "contains a medium & a séance"

#94    *Goosebumps* (series) by R. L. Stine
        "too gruesome"

#98    *I Saw Esau* by Iona Opie and Peter Opie
        "offensive illustrations"

#99 *Are You There God? It's Me, Margaret* by Judy Blume
"sex & anti-Christian behavior"

# Children's Classics and Why They Have Been Challenged

*Little Women* by Louisa May Alcott
"diminishes young women & fails to empower girls to succeed"

*The Prydain Chronicles* by Lloyd Alexander
"religious themes that are pagan"

*The Little Mermaid* by Hans Christian Andersen
"satanic pictures"

*The Wonderful Wizard of Oz* by L. Frank Baum
"religious viewpoint"

*Animalia* by Graeme Base
"violence & horror"

*The Five Chinese Brothers* by Claire H. Bishop
"violence & ethnic stereotypes"

*Alice's Adventures in Wonderland* by Lewis Carroll
"animals using human language"

*Charlie and the Chocolate Factory* by Roald Dahl
"poor philosophy of life"

*James and the Giant Peach* by Roald Dahl
  "profanity, alcohol, & smoking"

*The Story of Babar* by Jean DeBrunhoff
  "violence & 'pro-colonialism'"

*Strega Nona* by Tomie DiPaola
  "witches & witchcraft"

*Harriet the Spy* by Louise Fitzhugh
  "teaches children to lie, spy, & back-talk and curse"

*Anne Frank: The Diary of a Young Girl* by Anne Frank
  "sexually offensive"

*Complete Fairy Tales of the Brothers Grimm* by Jacob & Wilhelm Grimm
  "racism & violence"

*Hansel and Gretel* by Jacob Grimm & illus. by Lisbeth Zwerger
  "acceptable to kill witches & paints witches as child-eating
  monsters"

*Little Red Riding Hood* by Jacob Grimm & illus. by Marjan Van Zeyl
  "violence & child taking wine to grandmother"

*The Phantom Tollbooth* by Norton Juster & illus. by Jules Feiffer
  "poor fantasy"

*The Just So Stories* by Rudyard Kipling
  "racial slurs"

*The Lion, the Witch and the Wardrobe* by C. S. Lewis
  "graphic violence, mysticism, & gore"

*The Story of Doctor Doolittle* by Hugh John Lofting
  "expurgated in the 1960s to conform to changing sensibilities"

*Mother Goose: Old Nursery Rhymes*
  "anti-Semitic verse"

*My Friend Flicka* by Mary O'Hara
  "bitch in reference to a female dog"

*Froggy Went A-Courtin'* illus. by Kevin O'Malley
"nefarious activities, including burning money & speeding away from the Cat police"

*Green Eggs and Ham* by Dr. Seuss
"homosexual seduction"

*Winnie the Pooh* by A. A. Milne
"talking animals are 'insult to God'"

*The Lorax* by Dr. Seuss
"criminalizes the forest industry"

*The Giving Tree* by Shel Silverstein
"sexist"

*Eloise in Paris* by Kay Thompson
"nude artwork"

*The Lord of the Rings* by J. R. R. Tolkien
"smoking & irreligious"

*Charlotte's Webb* by E. B. White
"talking animals are blasphemous"

*The Happy Prince and Other Stories* by Oscar Wilde
"distressing & morbid"

*Little House in the Big Woods* by Laura Ingalls Wilder
"promotes racial epithets & is fueling the fire of racism"

*The Rabbits' Wedding* by Garth Williams
"interracial marriage"

# Caldecott Medal and Honor Books: Why They Have Been Challenged

## CALDECOTT MEDAL WINNERS

1995    *Smoky Night* by Eve Bunting & Illus. by David Diaz
        "violence & horror"

1985    *Saint George and the Dragon* retold by Margaret Hodges & illus.
        by Trina Schart Hyman
        "violence & horror"

1970    *Sylvester and the Magic Pebble* by William Steig
        "animal characters, pig policemen & magic"

1964    *Where the Wild Things Are* by Maurice Sendak
        "dark & frightening"

1941    *They Were Strong and Good* by Robert Lawson
        "glorifies slavery & racism"

## CALDECOTT HONOR BOOKS

1992    *Tar Beach* by Faith Ringgold
        "racial stereotype & the adults drink beer"

1984    *Little Red Riding Hood* by Trina Hyman
        "bottle of wine in girl's basket"

1982    *Outside Over There* by Maurice Sendak
        "frightening"

1977    *The Amazing Bone* by William Steig
        "graphic & detailed violence"

1971    *In the Night Kitchen* by Maurice Sendak
        "nudity"

1956    *Crow Boy* by Taro Yashima
        "promotes racial separation"

# John Newbery Medal and Honor Books: Why They Have Been Challenged

## NEWBERY MEDAL WINNERS

2007   *The Higher Power of Lucy* by Susan Patron
       "sexual content, specifically the word scrotum"

2000   *Bud, Not Buddy* by Christopher Paul Curtis
       "profanity/language & violence/horror"

1996   *The Midwife's Apprentice* by Karen Cushman
       "not appropriate for middle school students"

1995   *Walk Two Moons* by Sharon Creech
       "depressing"

1994   *The Giver* by Lois Lowry
       "sexual content & euthanasia"

1992   *Shiloh* by Phyllis Reynolds Naylor
       "profanity & lying & religious viewpoint"

1991   *Maniac Magee* by Jerry Spinelli
       "racism"

1981   *Jacob Have I Loved* by Katherine Paterson
       "offensive language & moral/religious grounds"

1979    *The Westing Game* by Ellen Raskin
        "violence"

1978    *Bridge to Terabithia* by Katherine Paterson
        "profanity, negative views of life, & witchcraft"

1977    *Roll of Thunder, Hear My Cry* by Mildred D. Taylor
        "racism & language, specifically the word 'nigger'"

1974    *Slave Dancer* by Paula Fox
        "too graphic depiction of the slave trade"

1973    *Julie of the Wolves* by Jean Craighead George
        "sexual content & violence"

1970    *Sounder* by William Armstrong
        "language, specifically the word 'nigger' and the word 'boy' in
        reference to a black sharecropper"

1969    *The High King* by Lloyd Alexander
        "religious themes that are pagan"

1963    *A Wrinkle in Time* by Madeleine C. L'Engle
        "witchcraft and undermines religious beliefs"

1959    *The Witch of Blackbird Pond* by Elizabeth George Speare
        "witchcraft and culturally offensive, specifically the word 'squaw'
        in reference to a Native American woman"

1951    *Amos Fortune, Free Man* by Elizabeth Yates
        "racist dialogue, stereotypes"

1944    *Johnny Tremain* by Esther Forbes
        "violence"

1923    *The Voyages of Dr. Doolittle* by Hugh Lofting
        "expurgated in the 1960s by publisher to make the books con-
        form to changing sensibilities

## NEWBERY HONOR BOOKS

2005   *Al Capone Does My Shirts* by Gennifer Choldenko
"profanity"

2004   *Olive's Ocean* by Kevin Henkes
"sexually explicit & profanity"

2003   *Hoot* by Carl Hiaasen
"profanity, including damn and smartass"

2001   *Because of Winn Dixie* by Kate Di Camillo
"profanity"

1998   *Ella Enchanted* by Gail Carson Levine
"adult content"

1996   *The Watsons Go to Birmingham—1963* by Christopher Paul Curtis
"racism, political view, & language"

1996   *What Jamie Saw* by Carolyn Coman
"profanity & inappropriate language"

1995   *Catherine Called Birdie* by Karen Cushman
"anti-Semitic values"

1994   *Crazy Lady* by Jane Leslie Conly
"swear words, specifically damn, hell, and bitch five times"

1992   *Nothing But the Truth* by Avi
"profanity & inappropriate language"

1990   *Shabanu: Daughter of the Wind* by Suzanne Fisher Staples
"sexual content"

1988   *After the Rain* by Norma Fox Mazer
"profanity & sexual content"

1988   *Hatchet* by Gary Paulsen
"graphic depiction of trauma"

1987   *On My Honor* by Marion Dane Bauer
"profanity & depressing"

1985   *Like Jake and Me* by Mavis Jukes
       "sexual content"

1985   *The Moves Make the Man* by Bruce Brooks
       "violence"

1984   *The Sign of the Beaver* by Elizabeth George Speare
       "culturally offensive, specifically using squaw for Native American woman"

1979   *The Great Gilly Hopkins* by Katherine Paterson
       "profanity & graphic violence"

1977   *Abel's Island* by William Steig
       "references to drinking wine"

1976   *Dragonwings* by Laurence Yep
       "graphic violence, profanity, alcohol/drug use"

1975   *My Brother Sam Is Dead* by James Lincoln Collier
       and Christopher Collier
       "politically, racially, & socially offensive"

1975   *Summer of My German Soldier* by Bette Greene
       "profanity, negative views, & offensive racial stereotypes"

1973   *The Upstairs Room* by Johanna Reiss
       "profanity"

1973   *The Witches of Worm* by Zilpha Keatley Snyder
       "the occult & fantasy about immoral acts"

1972   *The Headless Cupid* by Zilpha Keatley Snyder
       "occult & Satanism"

1966   *The Egypt Game* by Zilpha Keatley Snyder
       "occult, condones trespassing & lying"

1942   *Little Town on the Prairie* by Laura Ingalls Wilder
       "offensive to Native Americans"

# Index